The
Storekeeper's
Daughter

The Storekeeper's Daughter

A Memoir

Katie Funk Wiebe

HERALD PRESS
Scottdale, Pennsylvania
Waterloo, Ontario

Library of Congress Cataloging-in-Publication Data
Wiebe, Katie Funk.
    The storekeeper's daughter : a memoir / Katie Funk Wiebe.
        p. cm.
    ISBN 0-8361-9062-9 (alk. paper)
        1. Wiebe, Katie Funk—Childhood and youth. 2. Mennonites—Canada—Biography. 3. Russian Germans—Canada—Biography. 4. Children of immigrants—Canada—Biography. I. Title.
    BX8143.W43A3 1997
    289.7'902—dc21
    [B]   96-49369

The paper used in this publication is recycled and meets the minimum requirements of American National Standard for Information Sciences— Permanence of Paper for Printed Library Materials, ANSI Z39.48-1984.

All Bible quotations are from *The Holy Bible, King James Version.*

THE STOREKEEPER'S DAUGHTER
Copyright © 1997 by Herald Press, Scottdale, Pa. 15683
        Published simultaneously in Canada by Herald Press,
    ·Waterloo, Ontario. N2L 6H7. All rights reserved
Library of Congress Catalog Number: 96-49369
International Standard Book Number: 0-8361-9062-9
Printed in the United States of America
Book design by Paula M. Johnson/Cover photo of the author from her files.

06 05 04 03 02 01 00 99 98 97 10 9 8 7 6 5 4 3 2 1

*Dedicated
to my grandchildren
Matthew
Christiana
David
Jamie
Jennifer*

*to give them a better understanding
of their rich heritage*

Contents

Author's Preface

M Y PARENTS GAVE me many gifts during their life-times. Which gifts do I still treasure? Even remember? The golden-haired doll dressed in an old-fashioned gown edged with mauve lace, which I received when I was about eleven or twelve, lies in the bottom of my trunk waiting to become an antique. I no longer have the fuzzy electric-blue housecoat with the long, long zipper (zippers were new then) which made me feel like a British princess.

The better gifts didn't come at Christmas, nor did they come gift-wrapped. They came in the form of stories told around the oilcloth-covered table on a winter evening—childhood experiences in Russia, funny stories about working in a mental hospital, courting during the Russian Revolution. Some were sad stories about war and famine, courageous ones about immigrating to America with only a samovar, a flour sack filled with roasted rolls and six polka-dotted diapers for my baby sister. Stories were as much a part of our lives as the homemade bread we ate.

Literary critic Alfred Kazin once told a conference of English teachers that the immigrant writes "to make a home for himself [or herself] on paper—to find a place, a ledge." The newcomer tells stories to identify a once-secure place: "This much I know about myself. . . . this part of my life is secure. I can talk about it. Now how do I match this new experience that I yet don't understand with what happened?"

Kazin spoke particularly about the immigrant child (he was one). "Language is the salvation of the immigrant who

9

must reorder his or her existence by means from within." Immigrants have only language by which to pass on what is important to them. The past is gone, often along with family heirlooms and other artifacts. The territory in the new land is new. Immigrants have only memories, a value system, and hope for the future. The only way to pass on the values inherent in their past and to explain the reason for making a break with it is through stories.

My father was an immigrant who told many stories. He worked hard at dealing with the experiences of his yesteryears—war, revolution, death, famine, migration, lack of education, a sense of inferiority, a church in flux. Some stories he carried with him into the grave.

I sense now it took courage for him to release some of those stories. Such stories of faith and joy, but also of hopelessness and despair, shaped my life but also unlocked my own dreams. I learned that success may not always be readily achieved, but the reaching is important.

A life story provides a pattern. My father's stories showed me how values became living truth in another time and setting. My identification with the emotions involved in his story gave me insight and opened the way to a more mature faith. Equally important, his stories gave me permission to risk telling my story. Persons who never get a chance to tell their stories lose out if storytelling isn't welcomed and cherished.

I know the writing of these stories may not stop a riot, but I hope they will help all readers, young or old, to understand the gift of their heritage. A knowledge of my past helped me understand how to face an uncertain future. I hope my stories will help all readers to grasp that as human beings we always face uncertain odds. Stories of the past show us how to deal with the present.

A story is a gift, a hug, a way of embracing another person. These stories are my gift to you, the reader. Some of you have asked for them. They are selective, dealing with only some of my experiences from early childhood through high school. The essential elements are true. Some names have been changed. To convey this truth, I have used the fictional mode. Some stories have appeared in other publications and are gathered here to bring them home.

—Katie Funk Wiebe
Wichita, Kansas
March 1996

Acknowledgments

WHEN I COMPLETED this manuscript, I was overwhelmed by the number of people who had made it possible: all the people who were part of my childhood—my mother and father, sisters and brother, relatives and friends across the river and across the ocean, and the villagers of Blaine Lake, both young and old.

I value the critical comments of my sister Anne Kruger and my daughter Christine Wiebe who read the original manuscript.

I cannot fail to mention the many people who heard some of my stories and encouraged me to get them published.

I appreciate the positive response of Herald Press editor Michael King and the book evaluation group who were willing to look at my manuscript and encouraged me to finish it.

Many of these stories have appeared in print in various publications: Parts of "Final and Fatal," in *Good Times with Old Times*; Chapters 3, 4, and 5 in *Journal of Mennonite Studies*, 1995; parts of "The Storekeeper," "The Storekeeper's Daughter," and "Going Down Main Street" in *Good Times with Old Times*; parts of "Waiting for Summer" and "Becoming a Woman" in *The Christian Reader* and *Growing Up in Blaine Lake*; "A Real Live Death," in *Liars and Rascals: Mennonite Short Stories,* University of Waterloo Press and in *Breaking Through: A Canadian Literary Mosaic Grades 11 & 12*, Prentice-Hall Canada, Inc. A number of short episodes have been published in *The Christian Leader, Mennonite*

Brethren Herald, and *Christian Living.*

Sources in addition to my own memory and notes:

Personal interviews with my parents, Anna and Jacob Funk, now deceased, and with some of my siblings, as well as letters and writings by my father.

Blaine Lake 1912-1962 (Golden Jubilee publication). Blaine Lake, Sask.: Jubilee Book Committee, 1962.

Welcome to Blaine Lake 1980 (75th Anniversary publication). Blaine Lake, Sask.: History Book Committee, 1980.

Block, Neta Janzen with Katie Funk Wiebe. *Neta's Story.* Wichita, Kan.: Unpublished manuscript, 1995.

Crowder, Blanche. *Bridging the Years: Era of Blaine Lake and District 1790-1980.* Blaine Lake, Sask.: Town of Blaine Lake and Rural Municipality of Blaine Lake #434, 1984.

Epp, Frank H. *Mennonite Exodus.* Canadian Mennonite Relief and Immigration Council. Altona, Man.: D. W. Friesen & Sons, 1962.

Funk, Henry J. *The Funk Family Tree.* Self-published, n.d.

Funk, Jack, ed. *Growing Up in Blaine Lake by Five Who Did.* Battleford, Sask.: Self-published, 1991.

Funk, Jack. The story of Dad's imprisonment included in Chapter 11 was first heard and recorded by my brother Jack Funk.

Funk, Jack. *Jacob and Anna Funk 1920-1985.* n.p. Self-published. 1985 (Brief family history and copies of family documents).

Funk, Jack and Joyce. n.p. Self-published. *Those Were the Days*. 1983.

Funk, Abe. J. with Katie Funk Wiebe. *My Childhood in South Russia*. Wichita, Kan. Unpublished manuscript, 1994.

Hofer, D. M. *Die Hungersnot in Russland*. Chicago: K.M.B. Publishing House, 1924.

Lohrenz, G. *Sagradowka: Die Geschichte einer mennonitischen Ansiedlung im Süden Russlands*. Rosthern, Sask.: Echo-Verlag, 1947.

Neudorf, J. J. et al. *Osterwick 1812-1943*. n.p. Osterwick Publications Committee, 1973.

Schellenberg, Dave. *Reflections*. n.p. Self-published manuscript, 1972.

Schroeder, Gerhard P. *Miracles of Judgment and Grace*. Lodi, Calif.: Self-published, 1973.

Tiessen, Hildi J., editor. *Liars and Rascals: Mennonite Short Stories*. Waterloo, Ont.: University of Waterloo Press, 1989.

Wiebe, Katie Funk. *Good Times with Old Times: How to Write Your Memoirs*. Herald Press, 1979.

The Storekeeper's Daughter

1
A Letter from Russia

DOES THE road wind up-hill all the way?
Yes, to the very end.
Will the day's journey take the whole long day?
From morn to night, my friend.
—C. G. Rossetti

MOTHER EYED ME critically as I blew my nose and mopped up the drippings in an overworked hankie. I said nothing. I knew I would have to prop myself on pillows all night to find breath. Colds were tortures worse than scoldings for things I hadn't done. I sniffed hard, snuffling the phlegm back up my nose. The hankie was full.

"Get a clean hankie."

I examined my grungy one and threw it in the washing machine, which substituted as a laundry hamper between washdays. I went to the hankie drawer in the kitchen cabinet for another rag-hankie. Frieda and Annie could take store-bought ones to school—if there were any left after a series of colds had swept through the family. The drawer was just about empty, so I quickly hid a couple of colorful bought ones with cartoon characters under the pile of Dad's big hankies. That way I'd be sure to have some if the laundry for this week didn't get dried on time.

We sat around the round dining room table, Dad checking his store accounts, Mother darning socks from the never-ending pile or knitting and listening with one ear to Annie and Frieda read from their readers. First Annie read the ballad of "The Wreck of the Hesperus," which I liked, in which the skipper took his little daughter to sea and both drowned. Then Frieda read "The Slave's Dream." When they finished, Mother picked up Frieda's book and read the poem out loud to them. She could read English almost as well as they could —sometimes.

"And it passed, like a glorious roll of drums, troo da triumph. . . ."

"Through the triumph," Frieda corrected.

Mother tried again: "Troo da triumph. . . ." Then she shifted to the more comfortable Low German. "I can't say it—my tongue is too short. See—" and she stuck it out to show she couldn't get it past her bottom lip. "I never could stick my tongue out at anyone." She chuckled. "I'm tongue-tied. Someone forgot to snip the cord under my tongue when I was a baby."

I winced to think of a mother hauling out a pair of shears to slash that veiny section under the tongue so the baby could say "through" later in life.

Dad stopped his store bookkeeping long enough to pronounce the enemy words, but with little more success but for noise. "Anna, remember when we lived in Laird and I was taking English lessons from that Friesen—he said it wasn't tongue-tied—just your German tongue."

About thirty new immigrants had been taking English lessons from a fellow German who knew the language. The immigration department agreed to furnish books, pencils, and readers. But the immigrants didn't learn fast enough; their teacher wasn't strict enough and let them lapse into Low German. So he was released and an *Englischer* hired. Then they had learned.

The teacher said "ceiling" and the class said "ceiling."

She said "dog" and the class said "dog," not some German word. The next evening they went over the words again. And again. She dared their German tongues to say "three" and "those." They were to place their tongues behind their teeth and push the air through. She sat close to one of the men, explaining what she wanted. Though missing a few teeth, he was anxious to please, so he placed his tongue firmly against his few remaining teeth, blew hard, spraying the teacher's face with a blast of saliva. He was more shocked than she at what a courageous "th" could do.

"Me shamed," he stammered. The teacher wiped the spit off her face with her handkerchief and kept on. This mishap was all in the line of rescuing immigrants from remaining second-class citizens due to illiteracy. Dad liked to tell this story and the story about these adults who had stood in front of the class to read about Mama Bear and Papa Bear like first graders.

Mother read on about the slave in Egypt, stumbling over the big words and "th" words.

He did not feel the driver's whip,
Nor the burning heat of day;
For Death had illumined the Land of Sleep,
And his lifeless body lay
A worn-out fetter, that the soul
Had broken and thrown away!

"It's a long time since we've heard from Russia," she said, pushing the book from her and turning to her mending that was always by her chair. "No one has written for a long time—maybe they're busy. Last night I dreamt about my mother," she said to no one in particular. She was speaking in Low German, which at the age of four I understood better than English.

"I dreamt you walked into the bedroom with her," she said to Dad. "She looked so well, so happy. She seemed so real—I wanted to reach out and hug her. I said, 'How did you get here? Why didn't you tell me you were coming? I would have gotten something ready for you.' I woke up expecting her to be in the room—but she wasn't there." Her voice dropped to a husky whisper. I didn't really know all the relatives she talked about who lived far away.

"How come if Daddy's mother lives in Hague, your mother and father didn't come to Canada too?" asked Annie.

"Papa was afraid to cross the ocean," she said. "He'd read too many stories about the Indians—he was sure they'd kill him. My brothers said if they had enjoyed good times in Russia, they could stand the bad times, so they stayed. My mother was glad Dad and I could leave—but she found it hard to see us go."

She wiped her eyes with a rag hankie, which made me want to cry. She was speaking more to the older girls than to me. "Mama had many children—twelve—but she loved each one. They were always poor. When Papa could, he always brought each child a present after he'd been away—until the hard times—when there was nothing to bring—or eat. Mama said she felt as if she was burying us alive when we left for Canada five years ago." Her voice barely reached me.

The next day I sat at the kitchen table coloring, near where Mother was ironing. I heard Dad's sure footsteps crunching the fresh snow on the narrow wooden sidewalk next to the house. In northern Saskatchewan, snow frequently fell in October and stayed until April, the drifts around the house growing deeper and more solid with each storm. Dad rarely came home from the store except at mealtimes. His place was at the store as much as Mother's was at home.

Today he was moving quickly, but then I had never seen my father saunter. When he and my little red-haired mother walked together somewhere, he was usually a good three paces ahead of her, which was more a part of his nature than a desire to leave her behind. If something was happening, he had to be up front to know what was going on. She'd say, "Don't rush so."

He'd look back, perplexed, hesitate, and say, "I'm not rushing." This was true; he was going at his regular pace. He'd keep walking, looking neither to the right nor the left. He had to know whatever was there to be known and become involved in it, if involvement meant hard work like pushing, pulling, carrying, or dragging. He liked that. If involvement required nice words, fancy handshaking, and backslapping, he retreated.

I looked up from my coloring when Dad gave the wooden kitchen door, heavily ridged with frost, a quick shove and stepped inside, out of the cold. The door was always a little balky when the snow and frost on the outside and the heated moist air on the inside fought to control the threshold. He strode toward Mother with a troubled look on his face. He didn't bother to take off his cap first. He held the afternoon mail in his bare hand.

Mail was as important as daily food. On Tuesdays, Thursdays, and Saturdays, the mail arrived for Blaine Lake's three hundred inhabitants on the early noon train at the Canadian National train station. On the other days, it came shortly after three from the opposite direction, but with the same reception committee. Villagers who had nothing better to do stood around to see who was arriving and to guess what was bringing them, who was leaving, and what was taking them away from Blaine Lake. Going to meet the train was a necessary daily activity, like eating meals or going to the outhouse. You went because you had to.

The postmaster waited also with his small wooden handcart, as did the drayman with his horse-pulled flatbed on sleigh runners. Each man picked up what was designated as his and moved on. In half an hour or so, after the postmaster had sorted the mail, we could pick up ours in Box 26. Either Dad went for it or my older sisters collected it on the way home from school. They gave Dad his business mail and gave Mother the rest.

Occasionally, there was a letter and often a newspaper, church paper, or catalog. If the box was empty, we could still contemplate what might have come. Today was Wednesday, but Dad had not waited for one of the girls to pick up the mail.

He held out a thin letter edged with black ink to Mother. I had never before seen a letter with the strange dark border, etched with a pen, although I recognized it as one of those odd-shaped thin envelopes that came from relatives in Russia by the way it was stuck over with strange stamps and smudgy postmarks. Inside those envelopes were usually several pages of thin coarse paper covered with writing that looked more like hen scratching than what my sisters copied neatly in school. We received those letters from Russia at irregular intervals. They never meant as much to me or my sisters as a letter from a cereal company sending us the ring with the secret compartment we had ordered in exchange for our collection of box tops.

I stopped coloring. Dad cleared his throat. He started to say something, stopped, and tried again, shoving his heavy cap with the earflaps back first. Small lines tightened around his eyes. *"Deene Mama es jestorve."* Mother looked up with a jerk, stopped ironing, and wiped her hands on her apron. She always wore an apron, for it meant fewer dresses to launder.

What Dad had said meant little to me as I sat at the table listening. I had never met my mother's mother—my grandmother. I had no idea who this strange person they were talking about was.

"Oba nae!" She carried the sadiron from the ironing board to the stove and covered it with a beat-up rusted baking pan to keep it warm. She stood still, staring at Dad, face drawn, eyes big and shining.

"In her last letter, she wrote that she wasn't feeling well, but not too bad—how did it happen . . . ?"

Her tears flowed, and inside I felt a lump growing like the time I had to eat the gooseberry *Moos* I hated. She took the letter from Dad and sat down at the oilcloth-covered table across from me. Dad sat down too. She pulled the folded papers from the opened envelope and smoothed them out, looking for the first page. When she found it, she read softly to herself from the closely written sheet.

Dad got up for a minute, then sat down on one of the ivory wooden chairs, whose bare rungs always contrasted with the painted areas because we children hung our heels on them. He sat silent, troubled, looking at me without looking at me. I waited, the lump inside me getting bigger and harder by the minutes. The logs in the kitchen stove crackled and popped gently, out of tune with what was happening.

I didn't know what to think. We children knew Mother had parents and brothers and sisters far away just as Dad had a mother and grownup brothers and a sister close by—but because Mother's relatives lived in that faraway land of Russia, the relationship meant nothing to me.

We visited Grandma Funk in summer. She lived in the tiny village of Hague across the Saskatchewan River in a small, dull gray, unpainted building with hollyhocks and lilacs cluttering the front yard and a backless bench leaning against the ridged wall by the front door, like a bit of transplanted Ukraine. Mennonite homes on the steppes had benches outside near the door to sit on in the cool of the evening and flowers to refresh the eyes and weary body.

Grandma Funk always wore a long black dress with a white apron stretched over her fat stomach. And it was fat, really fat, for it jiggled when she laughed. Her dark hair, slightly graying, was pulled tightly back and pushed into a small doughnut bun, making her fat round face look even rounder and fatter. If it wisped loose, she pulled out her back comb, combed it through from the front, leaving ridges like a newly plowed field.

On Sundays when we visited her, she laughed and told stories about Dad's pranks as a boy, and how she had thrashed him with the *Malchbraat*, the board that separated shallow bowls of milk set out to let the cream rise. She made *Kakau* for us children to drink; it was thickened with flour, and developed a strange skin on top that clung to my lips like a spider's web and felt like a slippery worm when I gulped it down. But I drank it to make her feel good, for I liked this jolly grandmother. I laughed at her funny pronunciation of cocoa, and found myself saying "Kakau" over and over again after we'd been there, thinking about cows and cow pies and wondering why she added flour to thicken it. That I had no grandfather never bothered me. I assumed grandparents came singly, or not at all.

At three o'clock on a winter afternoon, the sun finishes its appointed task and darkness claims the day in northern Saskatchewan, but Mother left the coal oil lamps unlit as she strained to read the letter, even turning it around and around to decipher what had been written along the edges. I sat quietly on the wooden bench behind the table, no longer interested in my coloring, watching this drama of separation and death unfolding before me, not sure what was taking place.

A death in the family.

Finally Dad went back to the store, and Mother went back to ironing on the board she had laid over the backs of two straight-backed chairs. What else was there to do? She stoked the fire in the stove with coal she scooped from the battered hod beside it and reheated the sadirons. The black-edged letter lay beside her as she worked in her usual manner. Pillowcases and nightclothes were folded flat on the ironing board. Mother ironed the more visible outside garments, like shirts and blouses, on top of those to save energy.

From time to time she stopped to wipe her nose and eyes with another rag-hankie. The first lay sodden, the tears trapped temporarily by the worn threads. *Deene Mama es jestorve.* What was death? What was death when it happened thousands of miles away? Why did Mama cry? My lump now felt like gooseberry *Moos,* cooked turnips, and headcheese all being served at one meal in one big bowl, and all intended for me.

Annie was the first to return from school. She came bounding into the kitchen, her cheeks reddened by the cold wind, ready to tell Mother something about school. She stopped short as she saw Mother's red and swollen eyes. She hung her coat, scarf, and mittens on the hooks inside the door and took off her heavy galoshes. She didn't wear brown knee-high felt boots any more like I had to.

"Meine Mutter ist gestorben." High German was our language with our parents. English was used in school and on the street. Mother pointed to the letter edged with black. Those were enough words for now. Annie picked up the letter, noticed the black border, glanced at Mother's red-rimmed eyes, and said nothing. When Frieda came, she received the same brief news.

We children sat silently together around the kitchen table, looking at the Eaton's catalog in the growing darkness. We watched Mother struggle under the weight of her grief, unready and unable to help her. Even Jakie, awakened from his nap, sensed the heavy atmosphere and played quietly with his homemade blocks on the rag rug in front of the stove.

I had always thought mothers outgrew their mothers, left them behind like we did our too-small shoes, stockings, and dresses. I knew so little about this faraway grandmother in the Mennonite settlements in the Ukraine. Now I sensed dimly, as only children can, that grownup mothers had mothers and that sometimes mothers died. Those grownup mothers who cooked meals and boiled loads of laundry on the stove in copper boilers on Mondays, who sewed dresses and pajamas for their children and made them wash dishes, who sometimes scolded them until they cried or hugged them until they laughed, felt sad sometimes too. Even lonely.

Dad came home from the store for supper about six-thirty, stepping inside the porch quickly to keep out the blast of wintry air. Often the many late customers who came in the pre-supper rush delayed closing time. He looked at Mother with a sympathetic look—no more. He said little as we ate.

After the dishes were done, Mother read the letter to all of us, her voice breaking from time to time. It was from her father, Franz Janzen, who lived in the Mennonite colony in Sagradowka district, Ukraine. He wrote that his wife had died on October 30. We received the letter, written about a month later, on December 20, five days before Christmas.

On October 30, Mother's father had gotten up and told Mariechen, Mother's younger sister, "You will have to milk for Mama today, for she is sleeping." The letter was written like that with all the exact speeches. Grandmother Janzen was sick and had had a bad night. Half asleep, she had heard them talking and had called out, "Mariechen, hobble the cow to milk it. Then put the rope to tie the cow and the milking bench back in the same place when you finish."

Grandfather Janzen had made the breakfast coffee for the children and sent them to school. After preparing dill tea for his sick wife, he had gone outside to work, leaving little granddaughter Süschen inside. After a short while, a brother-in-law had come to ask about Grandmother's well-being. Together they had returned to the house where she was sleeping. Grandfather had said to Grandmother, "Tina, Heinrich is here." No answer. He touched her shoulder to waken her, but she did not respond. She was dead.

Little Süschen had told them, "Oma woke up and jerked funny and then looked at me with big eyes. She did this twice, and then fell back." The funeral had been held a few days later, but because some of the older children living away from home could not come on time, the grave had been covered temporarily with boards. When the last child arrived, the family had gone to the grave together, opened the coffin for a last look at their mother, held a brief memorial service, then filled the grave with dirt. Mother's sister would write more details soon, the letter said.

Mother folded the letter and returned it to the envelope, fingering it as she stared into the dark living room. A heavy silence wrapped itself around each of us as we moved into the evening routine. Even little Jakie and I seemed to feel the pain that separated us from one another. The girls took out their readers, but Mother, who usually listened readily, had no ear this evening for "The Song My Paddle Sings." Occasionally Dad and Mother talked quietly about the letter and about her faraway family or about their former life in the land of the acacia and fruit trees, watermelons, storks, and nightingales. Mother stopped occasionally to wipe her eyes.

Frieda asked cautiously, "What was your mother like?" She didn't say "Grandma" for she wasn't a grandma to us.

Mother rested her chin in one hand, the thumb and little finger supporting from below and the other fingers nearly covering her mouth. She thought a moment. "Always friendly. She was one of four children—from a rich family. But in the last years, my parents were always poor, very poor. Sometimes they didn't have enough to eat." Her voice broke.

"Does the letter say why she died?"

"Papa writes she died of colic—but she had to work too hard these last years—and they had such poor food after the Revolution. The house they were living in was too cold—not finished. She wrote she had been sleeping on the floor for some weeks this fall . . ." Mother shuddered as the wind whipped around the corner of our house, gained force, and shook the windows.

"Did she look like you?"

I examined my red-haired mother. Dad sometimes teased her, saying she was a hot-tempered redhead. But my sisters always said she had auburn hair, not red. Auburn sounded more—well, acceptable in Canada. I saw a short, slightly plumpish woman with the kind of softness that felt so good when she pressed me against her—no bony places to hurt.

"No, she had dark hair—always very thin. She'd had smallpox as a child, which hurt her throat. She couldn't sing or laugh loud—her voice was hoarse—pockmarks on her face."

I had only seen one person in my life with a face like that. What would it be like to have had smallpox and end up with a face full of pits and dips, even the eyelids, and the inside of the mouth? I slipped my tongue around the roof of my mouth to assure myself its smoothness was still there.

"Who will look after your father now?" I asked. Fathers needed mothers to take care of them like Mother took care of Dad and us.

"Papa writes that my sister Truda will stay for a while to help with the younger children."

Annie interrupted, "How many children are still at home?"

"Well, there's Mariechen, and Martha, and Truda, and . . ." She listed them. She had told us those names before, but always the next day I had forgotten those strangers. We knew them only through words on paper in a language we didn't understand well and were losing rapidly in this new country in our hurry to learn English.

The next morning began as usual. After helping Mother start the fires at home, Dad left early, about six-thirty, for the store down the street to stoke the basement furnace with shiny black coal from the dark corner bin to get the place warm for customers who showed up early.

Keeping the house and the store warm was a big job all winter, for the weather sometimes dipped to thirty degrees or more below zero for weeks on end. Sometimes if I woke early, I could hear Dad turning the grates in the big living room heater, using the handle that always lay beneath it, while Mother started the kitchen stove. If he made too much noise and dust—he often attacked a job with more speed and force than necessary—she would whisper loudly, *Schedde nijch zo*, and he would slacken his enthusiasm momentarily before carrying the ashes outside to the alley. Before long there'd be a warm spot on the oval braided rug by the big heater to stand on while I dressed for school. Then we'd have breakfast of hot porridge and milk with thick slabs of bread toasted in a very hot oven, making the outside of the bread crusty but the inside soft and warm.

As I woke I remembered the sadness that had rudely entered our home yesterday. I edged under the wool comforter again to feel for my personal bedstone, which by then had lost all its heat and lay there inert, giving no comfort to my feet. How did one grieve without a body, "that worn-out fetter, that the soul had broken and thrown away," to touch and look at? How did one sorrow without a grave?

Mother couldn't push aside the temporary boards to look into the coffin to say good-bye as her sisters and brothers had done. She had no way of contacting her father or sisters and brothers. There was no thought of jumping into the car, which sat on wooden blocks in the garage for the winter, and following the narrow sleigh tracks across the frozen Saskatchewan River to family and friends who might understand.

This sorrow was our sorrow. We six mourned. Two adults, four children. Not all of us understood what it was about, for death had to do with coffins and funerals and preachers—not black-bordered envelopes and milking stools. I had sometimes heard of people dying. I knew that little babies, tiny bits of humanity, died of diphtheria. Sometimes of other causes too, Mother said.

One day Dad told us that a man who lived down the street had been waiting for him at the door of the store when he got there. The man wanted a box, a wooden box. Most groceries were shipped in wooden boxes or strong cardboard ones.

"What for?" asked Dad.

"The wife had a baby last night—didn't live." He wanted a box to bury the infant in.

The family was poor, the poorest in town, Frieda said, to have to bury a baby in a packing crate. The children sometimes scurried barefoot from front door to back door, even in winter, the gossips relayed. We always wore slippers in the house, hand crocheted or knitted from old sweaters.

Dad had given him an empty wooden sardine box, which had held about twenty-five pounds of neatly stacked shiny tins of New Brunswick Sardines. These boxes made some of the best kindling to start a new fire. Sardines, kindling, coffin. Somewhere a little baby who had never cried once was rotting in the ground in a box marked "New Brunswick Sardines." Somewhere a tired grandma we had never known was resting in the ground from a life of toil and trouble.

I never knew how Mother worked through her grief. I was too young. Soon other letters arrived from her sisters giving more information about the funeral. Those people who wrote her were always her sisters—never our aunts. Then other letters came telling of other events in that country, a place that existed only in the words of letters—never as an accepted fact in my mind. I equated everything they wrote about dying, even hunger and exile, with the stories Annie and Frieda read out loud from their readers. I pushed it all away from me. Death was a fiction, a fantasy. I didn't expect to meet death close at hand.

2
Final and Fatal

HUMPTY DUMPTY sat on the wall,
Humpty Dumpty had a great fall;
All the king's horses and all the king's men
Couldn't put Humpty together again.

ONE DAY AT SCHOOL some snot-nosed English child informed me I was a Mennonite. To me, anyone who was not born of immigrant parents was English, even if the person was something else, like Irish or French. It had to have been an English kid, for they thought of themselves as being on top of the heap. I was about ten or eleven.

At noon I rushed home the three long blocks, taking the back alley shortcut behind Batanoffs' house and through the gap between Swystun's tailor shop and Koval's shoemaker shop to make it to our wooden gate in record time. My breath was steaming in the cold December air, and frost had formed on the scarf tied over my mouth. Once inside the door, I asked Mother the question on my mind.

Ja, Kind, wir sind Mennoniten, Mother replied.

She had never withheld this information from us. I knew that. I knew what her answer would be. I had heard the word *Mennoniten* often in the stories Mother and Dad told us about their earlier life in Russia. We attended a little white Mennonite church across the North Saskatchewan River.

However, to be pronounced a Mennonite by an outsider seemed so final—almost as final as the eternal hellfire the preacher shouted about at the revival meetings we sometimes attended in summer when the roads were open. Final and fatal. I was a Mennonite, whatever that meant. Someone had defined me, put me into a category, like a pumpkin at the fall fair.

Mennonite. Katie is a Mennonite.

But Becky hadn't said it as if I were getting the blue ribbon.

During morning recess we girls had discussed nationalities in the cloakroom. Sleek, black-haired Becky had said, "I'm Russian." Elaine, who sat in the seat ahead of me, her wool sweater bulging at the waist as usual and her kneed stockings hanging like balloons over her felt boots, added, "My dad says we're Scottish." A few more Russians, a Ukrainian, and a French girl spoke up before it seemed to be my turn.

I had hesitated, searching for an answer. What were we Funks? Mother and Dad spoke German as well as Russian, especially if they didn't want us children to understand. Dad could speak Ukrainian and a little Polish too, he said. I prided myself on my multilingual father. But my parents' English wasn't very good. They'd say, "Mrs. Horst, she coming today," or "The doctor thing, whatcha call it . . ."

Before I could say something, Rebecca, leaning against the doorway, singsonged loudly so all could hear, "Katie is a Mennonite!" At that moment the bell rang for classes to resume, and I followed the troop of girls out of the cloakroom back to our seats.

I was troubled by Rebecca's words, troubled through arithmetic and reading, troubled until the noon bell rang and I could dash home. We went to a Mennonite church like Evangeline went to a Catholic church, but she had said she was French, not Catholic. I didn't wait to walk with anyone as I usually did. When I asked my question, Mother gave me an answer I wasn't prepared to receive.

I forced down the macaroni and sausage Mother had prepared for us. Mother was always at home waiting for her family to come to her from the outside. She seldom went visiting or to clubs or things like that. Mother was the home person and always had a meal waiting. Over the meal we told her what we had been doing that day in school.

Mother worked at home cooking, cleaning, sewing, and mending. Mother worked and waited. I thought all mothers did only that. She never went shopping, except once in a long while if we didn't bring her exactly what she wanted or if something needed fitting. There was no such thing for her as weekly shopping for groceries either. It was a daily meal-by-meal affair because the store was so close. She'd be making the fire for supper and turn around to one of us children and say, "Tell Dad to give you a can of salmon." If she was sewing, she might say, "Get some money from Dad at the store and buy some elastic from Lubin's store before it closes."

Mother rarely handled money, except for small change. Money was Dad's domain, hers was keeping the household going. For that she needed little money. Frequently Mother gave us a before-school errand: "Get ten cents from Dad for two pounds of hamburger at Perrin's butcher shop. Tell him I want good hamburger." *Good* meant made with lean scraps, not fat ones. That Mrs. Funk knew her hamburger was implied in the way we were expected to lean on the word *good*. So we'd ask for GOOD hamburger and Mr. Perrin, a man of few words, would nod assent.

Dad had come home from the store for the noon meal. We always called it dinner. He was telling Mother something about an orchestra forming in the Russian Baptist church after Christmas. Perhaps Frieda, my oldest sister, could go and learn to play the striped, round-bellied mandolin hanging in the closet. Dad had received it last year from a customer who couldn't pay his bill.

Frieda made some comment. I wasn't listening. I was mulling over the morning's cloakroom discussion and wishing I could ask Mother some more questions. If all the other girls knew what they were, why didn't I? Was Mennonite something terrible and catching; or fatal like diphtheria, scarlet fever, or tuberculosis; something that you didn't talk about? Why didn't we talk more about Mennonites at home, so I didn't have to wonder about the word before I said it out loud?

After dinner and dishes—it was my turn to dry—I trudged back to the two-story, red-brick schoolhouse at the far edge of the village. The snow path, single lane, had already been packed hard by countless feet. The cold wind whipped around my toque, short coat, and brown lisle stockings. I dug my head deeper into my collar, not quite knowing what to do with this new knowledge.

At my desk I traced the deeply gouged markings of dozens of previous students, gave my inkwell a little rub (I always kept mine washed and clean), straightened my pencils, and began the writing assignment. I looked at Becky across the aisle. How did she know who I was?

Becky's parents lived in the center of town and her father was the doctor, a short, squat man with a toothbrush mustache, who came into the store often to talk with Dad. They were Russian, High Russian, Mother had once said. Their relatives had been important people in Russia. There again, Mother knew about Becky and Becky knew about me, but I didn't know about me.

Why weren't we Russian like the Nesdolys, or Ukrainian like the Slywkas, who had come from the same part of the Ukraine as Mother and Dad had? Somehow it didn't seem right to say we were German, or even Dutch. Our passport said we were Russian, but Mother said we weren't.

When Dad was eligible to be naturalized, he went before the judge trembling. His English wasn't very good yet, despite the English lessons. There was lots about this big country he still didn't know. He was afraid the judge would ask questions he couldn't answer.

"Is that your name?"

"Yes."

"Are you Russian?"

"No, I'm Mennonite."

"You were born in Russia, therefore you are Russian." The judge looked up from the documents Dad had presented. "How are the roads?"

"Good."

The judge was satisfied that Dad understood English and so he gave Dad the naturalization papers for Mother, Frieda, Annie, and himself, all of whom had been born in Russia. They were now Canadian citizens. And Russians. But also Mennonites. What the judge had said didn't really matter. He didn't know about Mennonites—that they were branded with a mark when they slipped out of the womb, a mark that superseded all other identities.

But what was Mennonite? Was that a religion, a nationality, or both—or neither? Maybe we were some strange new category. That thought was even more frightening.

Miss MacDowall, our grade two teacher, walked up and down the aisles watching us work. Usually she sat in her chair at the front as much as possible, because she was fat, fatter than my mother by a long shot. You could tell her feet hurt by the way she shifted her weight from one leg to the other when she stood at the blackboard. She wore flowery dresses made of sheer, summer-weight fabric. The dresses slithered around her body and seemed out of place with her shiny black oxfords tied with neat square bows.

That day her feet must have been feeling good, for she was walking up and down the rows correcting or praising students. As she bent over my shoulder, I almost forgot to look for the dark tunnel down the front of her dress that fascinated us girls. We speculated what this tunnel actually was in the human anatomy and whether we would have one some day. Miss Anderson, the grade five teacher, didn't have one, but then, of course, when she bent over a student, her buttoned-up collars made it impossible to see anything. Luba, who had older sisters, told us she had heard that girls grew two big rounds of soft cartilage in front that were joined at first and which separated when you grew up, making this dark, wrinkled tunnel.

Today even the tunnel didn't interest me, nor the extra reading period, which always pleased me. I wanted school to end so I could go home to Mother. As we walked out the door of the classroom, Jennie asked if I could come over and play.

"I have to go home and ask first." Even then I knew what the answer would be. We couldn't go into other people's houses to play. Was that part of being a Mennonite, always staying a little separate? Mother said she didn't believe in her children making a nuisance of themselves elsewhere. She was always concerned that the other mothers might think she had sent us there on purpose to get us out from under her feet. However, she didn't mind if other children came to our place to play anytime, which didn't always make a lot of sense to me. In summer our yard was full of kids because we had a playhouse, sandbox, teeter-totter, and two older sisters who could dream up exciting new games.

"Then walk home my way . . ."

I knew Mother expected me at home. We were often reminded to come home immediately after school unless we had monitor duty. It seemed natural for her to spend most of her time in the one-and-a-half-story frame house, built nearly on top of the slatted sidewalk in the front. She expected us always to tell her our whereabouts if we weren't at school.

Jennie and I pushed against the wind on the short block to her house without getting onto the topic on my mind that gave me courage to come this way. Perhaps Jenny could tell me what I wanted to know.

As Jennie turned into her gate, her mother, coming from Main Street, saw me and said, "Come in for some bread and jam, Katie." I saw wrapped bought bread sticking out of the bag under her arm.

Could I handle a two-minute delay? Sometimes the teacher asked me to clean the blackboards and Mother never minded. I stepped into the doorway, keeping the door slightly ajar so it would seem that I hadn't gone all the way inside.

Jenny's mother pulled two slices of bread out of the wrapper, spread butter on them, then strawberry jam, and gave Jennie and me each a slice. I didn't dare take off my coat, even though I was feeling sticky warm inside their kitchen where the fire was crackling loudly.

I sunk my teeth into the wonderful softness of bought bread and looked at the teethmarks I had carved into the butter. We only used one spread at a time in our home—butter or jam, never both. I ate away the soft crusts first, then attacked the center section. Bought bread during the week was a rare treat. We always ate big homemade loaves with heavy crusts that dried harder than shoe leather by the end of the week.

I rushed home, figuring out on the way what I would tell Mother if she asked where I'd been. The conversation would probably go something like this, she in German, I in English.

"Did you ask for something to eat?"

"No, of course not."

"Then why she gave you some bread?"

"She asked me to come in and have some bread. She said she wanted me to have a piece."

"You didn't beg for it?"

"Uh-uh," with emphasis.

But as I walked into the door of the lean-to kitchen, Mother told me she needed sausage for supper and to "quick run" to the store before I took off my coat and boots. The expected inquisition was postponed along with my chance to ask my questions. By the time I returned, Frieda and Annie were home, and I had to play with Susie and Jakie. Soon it was time for supper, and the seven of us filed in around the small kitchen table—three on a bench with our backs leaning against the wall, two on chairs on the other side, Mother and Dad at the ends. Nearby stood the wooden rack of frozen clothing, brought in from the outside by Frieda and Annie; it give off a sweet, fresh smell of the outdoors as it thawed.

For a few weeks, my being Mennonite stayed uppermost in my mind. I rehearsed the facts. We were Mennonites, yet my parents were born in Russia but spoke German as their main language. But Dad didn't like to be called a German. Sometimes he said we were Dutch. They had come to Canada in 1923 from the steppes of the Ukraine. That date became clearer in my mind. Why weren't we Ukrainians then?

Blaine Lake was homesteading territory which required strong bodies and souls ready to do hard work. Farmers came to town on Saturday evening to release their joy and grief and especially frustration. Occasionally brawling fist-fights erupted on Main Street. I hurried past to fulfill my errand (we were never on Main Street without a purpose) yet felt drawn to watch the raw emotion of these men lunging at one another, hollering obscenities, until the village policeman pulled them apart. Usually they were drunk. That was one of the earliest lessons I learned: Mennonites didn't drink. They didn't fight. If they did, there was something wrong with them—the Mennonite birthmark was wearing off.

Since churchgoing was important for respectable living and personal integrity, and since our own church was not represented in this community, we lived a double life. In summer we were Mennonite and attended services across the river, about twenty miles away. In winter we children were United Church—but that didn't make us United Church, like going to the Mennonite church made us Mennonite. Religion was more indelibly imprinted on Mennonites. It owned their souls, even if sometimes I felt like a rank worldling when we were dropped into that tightly knit Mennonite community across the river, especially at revival services. Hellfire evangelism was not a United Church thing.

We girls always traveled to the across-the-river church by car semi-ready—our sashes for our dresses neatly folded in a long flat box, and our hair sometimes in rags. At church Mother tied each sash into a big bow, removed the rags, combed our ringlets, and adjusted our hair ribbons. Dad gave us each a nickel. That was for the offering. There were two entrances side by side in this little white-frame church, one for women and one for men; it was not like at the United Church, where everyone entered by one door. In the Mennonite church in Laird the women sat on one side of the church and the men on the other.

Sometimes my father preached; sometimes the deeply tanned farmers who had been working in the fields all week expounded the Word of God. Dad preferred to preach among the Russians, he said, at the Baptist church near Blaine Lake. I never knew why until much, much later. It was part of an identity thing, which even he sometimes couldn't figure out.

After a day of visiting friends and family, we drove home late in the evening after the Christian Endeavor program (we always stayed for C.E.) or a revival service, three children slumped together in the back seat of the 1927 McLaughlin-Buick bought from Dad's employer at a discount. (It was a good buy, we were told. Buicks and Funks didn't really match.) Another child hunched on an improvised jump seat, and one squeezed between my parents while the car rattled homeward through the darkness on the rutty roads.

Mother always held the handle of the rear left door with one hand to make sure it wouldn't open and a child on her lap with the other. Sometimes Dad would sing *Heimatlieder* (songs about heaven) brought along from Russia, where the war-weary Mennonites had found comfort in an other-worldliness. As a child I grasped slightly the tight bond that pulled together all those who knew and found comfort in these songs. It came out of mutual longings for a better place where there was neither hunger nor sickness, sadness nor suffering caused by powerful people's inhumanity.

In winter, when the river froze over and the car was placed on blocks, all our Mennonite friends were forgotten for seven to eight months. We children switched to the United Church, and Mother and Dad became Russian Baptists. In later years, the Russian Baptist church moved into our house for Sunday services during the winter. The benches piled alongside the house were dusted free of snow, covered with blankets, and lined up in the living room. Many a Sunday noon, my sisters and I came home to the living room filled with benches, and grandpas and grandmas listening to the earnest tones of the Russian-speaking preacher who had no concept of time. We wondered when we'd get dinner.

In winter, we children did un-Mennonite things like skating (even on Sundays); enjoying a Santa Claus at the United Church Christmas program; joining the Canadian Girls in Training club; attending bake sales, minstrel shows, and amateur hours.

For a long time, our family was the only Mennonite one in the community, and I had all but forgotten what Rebecca had said that day in school. But periodically I was reminded what Mennonite meant. It constituted a bond stronger than blood ties among those who had shared the Mennonite experience of suffering in Bolshevik Russia. It drew them together. Little by little, I was sifting out what was Mennonite, never consciously but sort of like getting a tan. You find yourself turning browner but are never aware of it when it happens. Yet it did happen.

After we lived several years as the only Blaine Lake Mennonites, one day another Mennonite family moved to town. Mother and Dad then had some friends who were immediately closer than Blaine Lake friends. Some mystique drew them together. Then that family left but another Mennonite family soon came. Again Mother and Dad had friends who understood the meaning of *Mennonite*. However, Mother and Dad treated those newcomers to town with greater freedom of spirit. I sensed it at once. Those Mennonite friends were in a closer category than Russians or Catholics.

We weren't English—never. We weren't Russian either. We weren't Galicians or any of the other nationalities that had settled in our small town. Our neighbors were poor, but so were we. Once at a party at the doctor's house, I saw a copper coin on top of the piano. It was just lying there by a book. I stared at it in amazement. Money never lay around at our place, even a copper. But we were not the villagers' kind of poor. Even Mennonite poverty had a special quality. We never went on public welfare regardless how tight the money became. We wrapped our poverty in our moral integrity and struggled day-by-day.

Mother made clothes for us girls out of Dad's old pants and shirts. She made underwear, sheets, tea towels and tablecloths from flour and sugar sacks. Dad didn't smoke or drink, and we children weren't allowed near the pool hall, not even for a glimpse of its murky darkness. Somehow this frugality and integrity too were connected to being Mennonite.

The Mennonite mystique was slowly making its mark on me. My roots, whatever they consisted of, were reaching out and claiming me, and I didn't know it. I was burdened with the responsibility of piecing together the fractured parts of the whole.

3

"Peter Had Come Home"

A LITTLE old man of Derby
How do you think he served me?
He took away my bread and cheese,
And that is how he served me.

MOTHER HAD LOST her mother to death in 1928, but seven or eight years earlier, her whole family had been lost during the Russian Revolution and she was the only family member who pushed to try to find them. My father found them for her.

The story of how Dad found Mother's parents drifted into conversation often, yet it was made up of so many little stories that it never came together in one solid lump, like butter at the end of the churning process. I heard it as a very young child. I heard it when I was a young adult. I heard it as an adult.

The story always started with the statement, "Peter had come home." Usually Mother would say it, standing by the oilcloth-covered table washing dishes. As a family we rarely sat back in our chairs to talk after a meal. When supper was over, we did the dishes at once. To Mother there was something sort of obscene about having forks scabbed with egg yolk or untidy piles of chewed bones disgracing the plates. Very little time ever elapsed between eating and doing dishes. The two were one smooth operation with every child pressed into duty to clear, wash, dry, or sweep the floor.

Sometimes after supper, when we were sitting in our chairs staring at a clean table soon to be littered with schoolbooks and crayons, she'd say the words, "Peter had come home." Then she'd stop and stare into space. She had probably finished a row of knitting on a sock, which had required counting stitches, and she needed a breather. Peter was Dad's younger brother. Then, because that statement by itself didn't make much sense to us, Dad or Mother would start again with some other detail related to the story.

Eventually I realized the story about Mother's family getting lost and the story about my father finding them were actually two stories, maybe even three or more, that needed joining. The short statement about Peter coming home connected them like a bridge over troubled waters—at least in Mother's mind. Although the story was about Dad and her parents, it was actually her story, but she needed Dad's help with the telling of certain parts, because she hadn't been with him when he found them. She had been with little Frieda back in the village of Rosental, where they lived with his widowed mother and his younger brothers and sister.

But then, of course, no one thought of it as being a story in the true sense of the word, a story which needed a real beginning. How could there be a real beginning to an event that didn't have a real beginning like "Once upon a time some parents and their children lived happily in the village of Rosental in South Russia"? Life during the Russian Revolution (1917-1919) was not decisive like a scythe that brought a swath of hay to the ground in one swift stroke. Each day was a tangled mess of worries, fears, small joys, and troubled hopes amid the trauma of absent sons, fathers in prison or murdered, disease, hunger, and a whole family lost in the darkness of a land disturbed by revolution and anarchy.

The story was about her family, a family we didn't know

much about except for letters like the one that brought the news of the grandmother who had died lying on the floor of her unheated house and who, in her last moments, had said something about the milking rope and where to put it. The story was about that grandmother and what had happened a few years before her death.

The story of how Dad found Mother's parents began in the fall of 1917 when the Russian Revolution ended Russia's involvement in World War I. The Bolshevists overthrew the government and murdered the czar, who was related to the British royal family. One terrible night the czarist family was murdered, butchered—men, women, children, everyone. The thought made my skin clammy cold. I imagined the deep slashes gaping and widening, pouring forth their precious load of lifeblood. Then suddenly the pain broke through in quick stabs and longer waves, hurting, hurting, hurting, until finally strength was gone and death brought relief.

The Bolshevists wanted to take over the entire country. Russia was a big country to take over—I could see that on the map—but I guess they figured they could do it if they wanted to badly enough. The war between the Red and White armies continued for about two years all over the country, even where the Mennonites lived in the Ukraine. Yes, even where Dad's family lived near the noisy windmill with the big blades at the edge of the village.

The war front shifted back and forth through the villages in the area about nineteen times. How could anyone remember how many times the soldiers raged through the town with cannons, horses, and other kinds of artillery, then were forced to retreat? Wouldn't such moving back and forth get confusing? But nineteen times was the figure. Yet whether the Reds or Whites were in control, the villagers went to bed each night with fear, uncertain what the night and the next day would bring.

Dad came home from the Russian army in the spring of 1918, having finished his service as a medic on a Red Cross hospital train. Because he was not needed at home to help with the work in the mill, he volunteered to work as an orderly for several months at Bethania, the mental hospital about seven miles from Chortitza and from Rosental, where his parents lived. At the hospital he met and fell in love with a decisive, forward-looking, red-haired woman in a broad-brimmed green hat.

I liked to hear about the red hair and broad-brimmed hat, because then Dad and Mother looked at each other in a different way than when she was telling him to change his store smock. Dad would chuckle softly. He would look at Mother and smile broadly as if they shared a secret.

If it was early in the evening when the story of how Dad found Mother's parents was being told, we usually listened first to a few humorous stories about life in the mental hospital where both of them had worked or about the revolution. Dad made a big production of how after he returned home to Rosental he visited Mother at the hospital, about seven or eight miles away, where she was a cook. He bumbled through no-man's-land, cannon balls whistling between his legs as he ran to meet his true love.

After a few of these stories we still didn't know how Dad found Mother's parents—at least not that night—or even how they got lost. At ten o'clock it was always time to pull the chains on the clock, blow out the lamps, and go to bed.

Before Peter could come home, he had to go away. So that had to be explained first, and with that explanation came all kinds of other stories. In early September, Peter, Dad's younger brother, had joined the White army. Most Mennonites were opposed to taking up arms for any reason.

However, about forty or fifty zealous, young Mennonite men were upset with the war situation and were put under considerable pressure from a recruiting team which included at least one Mennonite. They agreed to enlist, but only for guard duty. They joined General Wrangel's White army. Only a few actually carried rifles, but the fact that pacifist families had sons in the government army angered the Red army leaders. They blacklisted each family and vowed to punish them. Of course, that was not something I figured out then—only years later.

To add to the Mennonites' troubles, fierce roving bands of anarchists under the leadership of Nestor Makhno took advantage of the unsettled conditions and the suspension of government control. They burned, plundered, murdered, and raped in what they spoke of as "acts of revenge" against the rich *Kulaks* of the area. In 1919 the Makhno bands made Chorititza their headquarters from September 21 to the end of December. That meant that Rosental, the adjoining village, was affected also. From these two communities, the bandits terrorized the area.

For over three months, the peaceful villagers lived in close daily contact with these swaggering, ruthless bandits who were always armed with rifles, revolvers, sabers, and hand grenades. They entered any home that had anything of value in it and took what tickled their fancy without questions. They were "liberating" these items from their former "filthy" owners. What they didn't value, they destroyed or spoiled. The villagers suffered emotional and physical abuse, first through threats, then through beatings, torture, sexual assault, and murder.

Such terrible goings-on were not mentioned to us children while we were growing up in the usually peaceful, occasionally brawling, community of Blaine Lake. I only sensed that buried deep in my parents' past were hurtful experiences too difficult to speak about.

Then one evening the mood would be set for the next episode. It would be bitterly cold as usual in those winters, with winds whipping around the corners of the house where the drifts were piled high, nails in the siding popping loudly from the cold. The fire in the big potbellied stove would have been crackling brightly for some time, causing us to pull back from it.

We'd probably had our fill of bread dipped in cocoa for our evening meal and were munching McIntosh apples brought up from the cellar. Maybe the family closeness as we sat together around the table or near the stove, maybe the feeling of security of being in a war-free country would trigger the memory of another family that had been lost during another chapter in my parents' lives in another country. Dad would begin and Mother would add the details he raced over, correcting and explaining, more for themselves than for us. Dad never had patience for long stories. He preferred the short, funny ones.

About September 1919, Dad had come home from Bethania Mental Hospital where he had been working for about seven months as a volunteer orderly. His father was sick with stomach trouble and Peter was in the White army, so Dad was needed to run the mill. Before he left the hospital, he and Mother agreed to marry as soon as the situation calmed down.

Terror stalked the village. Dad's younger brother came rushing home one day to say that he had gone into a house from which the owner had disappeared and had seen the owner's brains splattered all over a wall. He had probably resisted arrest. One evening a girl was gang raped in the family's living room, that was something Mother and Dad never talked about then. Dad and his brothers hid their sister under a table to protect her. Village men were taken to a brick building from which they never returned. The Funk family heard screams and sporadic gunfire coming from that building. At night they saw wagons loaded with corpses leaving it.

Dad's parents knew that sooner or later the revolutionaries would return. They didn't have long to wait. One day a number of armed riders galloped into the yard and seized Dad's father.

"Dark men, dirty—rough. I didn't like them," my father said.

Dad's father had harmed no one, but this small quiet man had to go. He was being taken hostage for having a son in the White army. Some soldiers butted him down the street. Several remaining soldiers shoved the other members of the family—Dad's mother, his sister, his three brothers, and Dad—against a wall and prepared to shoot them. But the lead man lowered his gun when an agitated rider rode up at full gallop and ordered the men to follow him. All the men jumped on their horses and left at top speed. The family had been saved.

Immediately, Dad's mother moved swiftly into action. "They will be back—they're not finished with us," she said. "Put on what clothes you can find, stuff the dried fruit into your pockets, and let's get away from here," she urged her children. With Dad's mother leading and her brood trailing behind, the family took off.

She didn't dare take the main road because the first army patrol would send them back. The little group trudged across fields, followed ravines, and pushed their way through bushes. When they got tired, they rested under a tree, always watching for soldiers. Eventually they arrived at the village of Kronstal where Dad's grandparents lived. Since they were not wanted by the revolutionaries in that village, Dad's mother figured they would be safe.

A few days later, who should arrive at Kronstal but Dad's father, a sorry-looking sight. He stumbled into the backdoor of the house, crying like a baby, at first unable to explain what had happened. Weary, clothes soiled and wrinkled, and emotionally exhausted, he told them that the soldiers had taken him two households down the street. With some other prisoners, they had stood him at the edge of a ravine running behind the property where the children used to play among the trees and bushes at the bottom. He begged them to let him go, for he had a wife and children at home who needed him. The men only jeered. "Your children can look after themselves, and we'll look after your wife. Let the runt have it."

A soldier aimed his rifle at him, but he could see the side of the rifle and knew the man would miss him. A bullet whistled past his head once, then again, and was followed by raucous laughing. The soldier was enjoying his cruel cat-and-mouse game.

The next time, he saw the rifle pointed straight at him and knew it was now or never. He threw himself backward into the ravine and took off. *They'll have to shoot me running,* he told himself. Immediately a rider was sent to the Funk home to get the other soldiers to help form a search party, but Dad's father was long gone. By saving his life, he had also saved his family.

He spent the night in the bushes. The next day he worked his way to a point where he could see the house. He didn't know whether other family members had escaped or were dead inside. He didn't dare investigate in case the soldiers were waiting for him inside. After watching all day and not seeing any sign of life, he decided to try the village of Kronstal where his relatives lived.

The vacant house in Rosental was an open invitation for the anarchists to move in and make themselves at home. Dad went back from Kronstal to check on the house periodically.

"I looked in the window of the kitchen," he told us after the first check. Cupboards stood open; doors were torn off, drawers emptied, and all household goods of value gone. Chests had been broken open; smashed dishes and chairs were strewn over the floor that was always kept so immaculate by Dad's mother. Bedding feathers formed a deep layer over everything, including the straw the bandits had been using to sleep on. He could see they had used the corners of the house as a latrine. Mud clung to everything. The livestock had disappeared. Only a few stray chickens scratched the dirt outside.

He returned a second time. The house looked deserted, so he walked in the open door, thinking the bandits had left it for a better place. While he was pushing the debris aside in the kitchen, looking for items of value, several bandits returned, sabers swinging, gleeful that they had found someone to harass.

Prodding his ribs with a knife, they urged Dad to tell where he had hidden valuables. Many people had buried money, clothing, dishes, and keepsakes to save them for a better day.

"I knew they had cruel ways of making people talk. I didn't think the torture was worth what I was trying to save, so I led them to the garden where I had buried, under the corncobs, a fur coat and some boots I had brought back from the army," Dad said. He had planned to use them when the war was over. He was tired of wooden sandals.

The bandits made him dig up what he had buried and carry it into the house for them. Then the dark-haired man with a heavy mustache, dressed in gaudy pants and shirt, and wearing high, polished boots, decided he wanted the fur coat. A feisty little fellow with fur cap cocked over his head and sabers and pistol dangling from his belt thought the coat should be his because it matched his headpiece. They argued, then fought, shoving each other around in the debris while Dad headed for the door, jumped the ravine, and dashed off. One bandit fired as Dad fled, but missed. Dad didn't go back to Rosental for a long time.

By December 1919, the Red Army had defeated the

White army and driven them into the Crimea. By the end of that disturbing year, the Makhno bands, though weakened by disease, also moved out, realizing the Reds no longer needed their unacknowledged support.

Though the village of Rosental was fairly safe to live in, for some peace and order had been restored, the Funk family still couldn't return. Typhus had spread to Kronstal. That and famine became the new enemies, rampant everywhere. Death visited many homes. Every so often a wagon would go down the street picking up corpses like garbage. Any man with strength left was enlisted to dig graves. The dead were usually buried three to an upside-down T-shaped grave to save energy. Various members of the Funk extended family took sick. Dad, who had had typhus in the army, helped nurse them.

On January 8, 1920, Dad's father, Johann Funk, weakened by his fall experiences, died of typhus. He was the first to go. He was still young at fifty-two. Before he died he whispered to his own brother Peter, still living at the parental home, that he had buried some money in the barnyard by the strawpile "third post from the corner." But everyone in the household, crowded with the refugees from Rosental, had too many other burdens to think about buried money.

That same day Dad's grandfather also died of typhus. These two men and a younger man from the village were buried in one grave three days later. Two days after that Dad's grandmother died and was buried with a man and another woman in the same grave. Then Dad's uncle Peter, who had received the message about the buried money, whispered it to Dad and died on January 21.

Four corpses in the house in two weeks. Dad, as the oldest male, had to be strong for everyone. For the rest of his life, he carried the scars of those weeks when death walked through the family and picked out the members he wanted.

"No one to help me." Even as a young child, I heard the

pain. All funeral arrangements were up to Dad. He had to see to getting the bodies washed and prepared for burial, coffins built, graves dug, and funerals arranged. His older brother John was married and not living at home, so there was no one Dad could turn to for help. His usual venturesome spirit suffered as he washed the bodies in the customary way and placed them on boards in the summer room, where bodies often froze stiff.

At the first graveside service, he asked a church elder to pray over the bodies before he filled in the grave, but the man wanted payment—half a load of manure for fuel, for he had sick family members in his own home. Dad had no manure to sell or give away. Where could he get manure at such a time? The deacon, a lesser church dignitary, came instead, free of charge.

After the next death, he asked a relative to help transport the coffin to the graveyard on his wagon. The man still owned some horses. Dad built simple coffins from slats ripped from the fence, for even lumber was unavailable. He had given another man a pail of wheat to dig the grave. But the relative with the horses said, "I'm too busy." Maybe he was.

But the body had to be buried. He placed it on a home-made wagon built with the wheels of an old plow—his younger brothers helped—and pulled the wagon to the graveyard at the edge of town, fearful each step of the way someone might have buried another body in the grave before he got there. At the graveside he lowered the coffin into the waiting hole, took off his cap, and recited Psalm 73:25-26, more for himself and his young brothers than for the dead: "Whom have I in heaven, but thee? And there is none upon earth that I desire beside thee. My flesh and heart faileth: but God is the strength of my heart, and my portion forever."

Then he filled in the hole, which now held its full quota of three bodies and went back to the land of the living. He did the same with the fourth body a few days later.

That story often ended there, with Dad saying to himself, "Yes, that's life—as long as a person doesn't have to suffer before he dies." When he had told about the coffins in the grave, Dad would get up quickly, check the doors, pull the weights on the clock in the parlor, and move in the direction of the stairs.

"We shouldn't have talked about it," he'd say on his way upstairs. The hurt was too great to dig around in often without opening festering wounds caused by lack of caring for those who suffered alone. To take with him into the waiting night the memory of how four people close to him had died within two weeks and how he had been undertaker, comforter, minister, and mourner was a test of his spirit each time he told the story. That and the memory of the weeping coming from his mother's bedroom as she faced a dark, uncertain future now that her husband, the wage earner, was gone. Where was the Defender of the afflicted, the One who had promised to save the children of the needy and crush the oppressors? Yes, where?

Peter had come home, but we still didn't know how Mother's family got lost and what his coming home had to do with them.

4

A Family Is Lost

LITTLE BO-PEEP has lost her sheep,
And can't tell where to find them;
Leave them alone, and they'll come home,
And bring their tails behind them.

*D*AD SAT AT THE dining room table working with bits of cardboard, some sewing machine needles, and an envelope.

"What're you doing?" asked Mother.

"Wait . . . just wait." He was impatient. Dad's method was to do first and explain later. If his plan didn't work, he didn't explain at all but threw everything into the kitchen stove.

That afternoon another of the scrawly letters had come from one of Mother's sisters exiled in Siberia, explaining that the last needle for her sewing machine had broken. The very word *Siberia* sent shivers down my back. I knew it only as a very bad place where the Russian communist government sent people it wanted to punish. Tina sewed for others to provide a little money for much-needed food. She had no money to buy another needle. The letter had only one message: Now even hope is gone. We must die.

The Russia letters came more irregularly during the thirties. When they arrived in our home, it usually meant Mother would cry silently for several days, and we children would talk more quietly and try to help more. Mother would tell us life in Russia was becoming more difficult for her relatives. Food was hard to get. Preachers, husbands, landowners, and others were being sent into exile, often into forced labor camps, sometimes prisons, never to be heard of again. Among those exiled were some of Mother's close family members—her sister Tina (whom we never thought of as an aunt) and her preacher husband. Mail to Russia was becoming uncertain.

For a number of years, Dad had been interested in pyramidology, drawing large and complicated diagrams of the huge burial places of the pharaohs of ancient Egypt, adding figures and measurements. Another local man, a British Israelite, had introduced him to this study, which promised to reveal facts and dates related to the endtimes. Obviously Dad had forgotten about his pyramids that night. That evening he pushed the needles into the cardboard and retrieved them. Then he pasted them between small sheets of cardboard and felt the little package. He was still not satisfied.

He got up and rummaged through the box of snapshots until he found one of our family beaming at the camera. He folded it in half just above the little children's heads and glued two needles in the crease. He had found the solution to the problem. He stuffed the folded picture and the letter Mother had written into an envelope and sent it off the next day. Months later word came her sister had received the needles. They had saved her life and the lives of her children.

When another letter came stating they had been without sugar for several months, Dad brought home a small bottle of saccharin tablets he had purchased at the drug store. Then he worked at the problem of how to smuggle these in a letter without arousing the attention of the censors.

I watched as he crushed the tablets to fine powder, then sprinkled the dust on the back of a picture smeared with mucilage, and topped it with another piece of cardboard. That too reached the Russian relatives. Sometimes he enclosed a dollar. If it got to Russia, it meant rye flour for two months, but Mother worried what they'd eat after that.

Her family in Russia had been lost once before and Dad had found them. Would they be lost a second time through starvation? That seemed to be the case, for there were fewer and fewer letters during the Stalinist years. So it seemed all the more important to Mother that we know something about these relatives whom we might never meet but who were part of our past.

So the story started again: "Peter had come home." We knew why he had been gone and where but not much more. The story still wasn't ready for the telling.

Mother and Dad had been thinking of getting married while they both worked at Bethania Mental Hospital, Mother as cook, Dad as an orderly. But times were unsettled. The Makhno bands, troublers of the land, made marriage plans impossible. They roamed the country. They were everywhere —at Bethania and also Rosental. At the hospital the kitchen staff sometimes fed up to fifty or more bandits each day for at least one meal at the command of the Makhno leader. The girls and women on the staff feared for their safety; the reputation of these men for abusing women preceded them.

Once during the long fall when little contact was possible, Dad walked from Kronstal to Bethania to visit Mother. The war front was never far away. For a time a cannon was set up in the yard of the hospital grounds. Late one night, standing on a bridge over a river, they arranged for an early spring wedding if "the Lord opened the way." Mother was attracted to Dad because he was concerned with "following the Lord" as she was.

On March 4, 1920, Dad's family moved back to Rosental from Kronstal, the place to which they had fled when the soldiers arrested his father. The old homeplace near the windmill on the high elevation at the edge of the village was in shambles—even the windows were gone. Though there was little straw or wood to burn in the big wall oven, they rejoiced that at least the fences were still in good repair.

Dad, his mother, three younger brothers, and a sister came to make a living there once again. Together they cleaned the house. They buried their clothing in the ground to disinfect it. They unpacked the household goods and bed linens they had brought along from Kronstal, where they were no longer needed now that both grandparents were dead. The mill was cleaned and the machinery repaired.

"What about the hidden money? Did anyone ever look for it?" I asked. That seemed a tidbit too exciting to leave out.

The following week Mother arrived in Rosental to visit and to make final arrangements for the wedding, only three weeks away. While she was there, Mother, Dad, and Dad's young sister drove to Kronstal with a horse and wagon to look for the money hidden on the old homeplace. Dad and a cousin living nearby waited until dark to start digging, for they didn't want to arouse the attention of neighbors or passersby. They dug deeply around post after post but never found the third post from the corner because the barnyard was a maze of corners.

Late in the night, when it was getting too dark to see what they were doing, they dug once more near a dangling fencepost close to the strawpile. They unearthed several milk jars full of czarist paper currency. But all of it was worthless because a new government was in control. Nevertheless, they divided it in case it regained its value in the future.

Dad took his portion back to Rosental and hid it under the cellar stairs. About a year later, when he wanted to show it to someone, he found a mouse had built a nest in it. He saved only a few rubles. His relative's life savings had made a mouse a comfortable nest.

Mother didn't know where her parents were; she had lost track of them during the revolution. So the wedding would be in Rosental, Dad's home community. On March 30, 1920, Mother and Dad were married in the Evangelical Mennonite Alliance Church by Mother's uncle, the head at Bethania and a minister. Nature provided a beautifully clear spring day as if to erase the memory of the horrors of the preceding winter. In front of a small congregation, they vowed to love each other until death parted them. They had exchanged rings earlier at their engagement.

"What did you wear?" I asked.

She couldn't buy herself the wedding outfit she had dreamed about as a girl. Yet she wanted to be married in a special dress, not just her old everyday one, so she remade the skirt of an old white voile dress, added a white blouse, borrowed a veil from a sister-in-law, and placed a wreath of green myrtle leaves on her head. Dad wore his older brother's wedding suit.

"I really looked nice," Mother said, smiling to herself and smoothing out her skirt.

"What did you eat at the wedding?"

It took additional ingenuity to make the wedding feast seem festive. A Seventh-Day Adventist man sold Dad some cabbage he had buried during the Revolution to keep the bandits from finding it. Mother used it to cook borscht without meat next door at Mrs. Penner's, who stayed home from the ceremony to keep it warm. When twelve guests arrived from church to eat the wedding feast at the Penners, Mother was chagrined. After all her careful arrangements, the soup was lukewarm—not piping hot as she had planned it and as it should be eaten.

"I called one of the serving girls from the kitchen and told her to take the big bowl of borscht back into the kitchen and reheat it—the guests would wait." Something like this could upset her. After all, she had a reputation as a cook to initiate among these new friends. Each guest received a bowl of borscht and piece of bread. After the meal the wedding party returned to Dad's home for the cereal coffee that Mother had made herself to be sure it wouldn't taste burned (the shame of a housewife) and zwieback baked with some available white flour. With that the nuptials ended. The young couple's only gifts were four or five small bowls from an aunt. But with each retelling of the story of the wedding, especially the food part, Mother would wax ever louder. "Can you imagine—serving the soup lukewarm?" To violate her standards of food preparation and service was a major felony.

It was most difficult for Mother to accept the absence of her parents and brothers and sisters on her wedding day. Her father had once told her, "Anna, as long as I have a piece of bread, you have a piece of bread." Did he have a piece of bread, even a small one, for himself and the rest of the family? Everyone—Mother, Father, Franz, Susie, Neta, Truda, Martha, Mariechen—had disappeared into the unknown after the revolutionary forces swept through their area near the Black Sea.

Her father, Franz Janzen, had been working as warehouse manager on a large Mennonite estate near Garletzky, close to the mouth of the Dnieper River, but rumors had reached Mother that the estate had been razed and all workers had fled. No one knew where. She had had no letters from her family for several years.

That estate, familiar to Mother because it had been her first main place of employment before going to Bethania, employed almost a small village in summer—up to two hundred laborers and household helpers and fifty shepherds. Therefore, its wealth was a prime target of the revolutionaries. She had last heard from her parents in 1917 at the beginning of the Revolution, three years before her marriage in 1920. She knew only that when the German army had crossed the Russian border during the war, her parents and their children still living at home had fled elsewhere to save their lives. She didn't know where.

"I told Dad I wanted to go find my parents." He replied, "Let's get married and then I'll look for them when times get better, if they don't show up beforehand." That promise became the pattern of his life: "If you hurt and I can help, I will."

Mother and Dad's home during the early months of married life was a small room in Dad's parental home, for he planned to continue working in the mill and helping his mother with the younger members of the family. His brother John was married and Peter was still in the army. His father's death barely two months before the wedding was still a raw wound.

In the spring of 1920, the villagers again had little seed for planting their crops, yet they worked the ground as best they could and planted the usual watermelons, potatoes, and other vegetables in addition to field crops. They rejoiced that, after the difficult winter, spring brought hope of better things. The blooming fruit trees were encouraging signs. In fall perhaps the high school and teachers seminary could be reopened—yet all these thoughts were tempered by the growing signs of collectivization and Russianization. The country was changing. It had changed from even a decade ago. The Mennonites no longer felt quite so at home in this country that had welcomed them warmly about 130 years earlier when they came from Prussia. The whole land seemed to be sneering at them.

Mother's concern for the whereabouts of her parents increased with each passing week. She had heard nothing but rumors about them for several years, and after she left Bethania, they didn't know where she was either.

Where could they be? Were they dead or alive? How had they died? Had the sharp swords of the bandits found them all, as was the case with other families in the area? When the ruffians had broken through the fences on their horses and rushed the big house, the barns, and the smaller houses, had her four younger sisters and two brothers been very afraid? Where were they?

There was little Mother, then pregnant, could do alone. Dad could not leave the windmill because his father was dead, Peter was in the White army, and his younger brothers were too inexperienced to take over. She waited and wondered as she worked alongside her mother-in-law each day, helping with the housework.

One morning in November 1920, before Mother was about to go down to the cellar for some potatoes for the noon meal, she moved toward the door to lock it to keep strangers out while she was below. Her mother-in-law was next door helping with the hog butchering, always a neighborly affair. As she was about to bolt the door, she saw a young man in army fatigues striding down the lane. She sensed something familiar about the way he walked. He kept looking at the house as he strode toward it. She stood by the window, wondering what to do. The young man walked resolutely down the stone-lined path toward the door, lifted the latch, and walked in.

"This must be Peter," she said to herself, as he prepared to greet her. Peter had been gone from home at the time of the wedding. Peter had been in the White army. Now Peter was home.

Mother ran next door to get her mother-in-law, who was deep into the morning's work, cleaning sausage casings. "Mama, Peter is home!"

The words electrified everyone, for some neighbors never expected to see him again. Quickly her mother-in-law washed her hands with water one of the girls brought her. She rushed home to meet her son. He was tired, dirty, and full of lice, but still smiling. Yes, Peter was home. The family rejoiced.

Dad could start looking for Mother's lost parents. But the

middle of November was no time to wander to unknown parts of the troubled country. Christmas would soon be here. The baby was not due until February, but the weather remained cold and unsettled. At the end of December, Dad was to be ordained as deacon and evangelist.

Peter's problems had not ended either. Within the month he was arrested and thrust into jail at Zaporozhe. Before he left his mother slipped a New Testament into his knapsack, for she knew he wasn't a believer and prison life was not easy.

Once again the waiting and praying for his release began. During the revolution Dad had done a favor for a Jewish friend, a member of the Red party, by informing him that the White army was moving into the village. "Hide," he had told his friend, "or the Whites will get you."

"Jake," said his friend, "I'll remember you some day," and he left the area until the Whites were defeated.

The Jews, bitter because of White pogroms and confiscation of their lands, had joined the Bolshevists. Now that the Reds had imprisoned his brother, Dad decided to find out if his credit with his friend was still good. Dad went to him one night asking for the release of Peter, who no doubt would be shot for volunteering for the White army. The friend recalled his promise and engineered Peter's release.

So Peter again came walking down the lane toward home.

"We thought it was an answer to our prayers," said Mother. That morning they had prayed again for his quick release, and before they stood up from the breakfast table, he was at the door. He was smiling his usual quiet smile and was ready to tell them that in prison he had read the New Testament his mother had stuck into his bag. As he had daily endured the screams and pleadings of other prisoners being taken out to be shot, he had thought he had but a short time to live. He had to settle matters between himself and God. In his prison cell, he had placed his trust in Christ, the Son of the living God. When the soldiers called his name, he was convinced his time had come, but he was ready. Instead the officer said, "Funk, take your belongings and get out." Together the family thanked God for bringing Peter home a second time.

Usually that was enough for an evening's storytelling. Someone would collect the apple cores and toss them into the fire which was barely glowing. Mother would throw on another hod of coal and close the dampers for the night. The finding could begin. It would begin. It only lacked the right moment for the telling. After all, Peter had come home.

I had learned many things about that distant past, not as far removed from the present as I had once thought. I knew why Mother shuddered if we talked about bedbugs or mentioned we had found a squashed louse between the pages of a borrowed book. Such creatures belonged to the past—an ugly, dirty, violent past. They were to be forgotten and left behind in Russia. They did not belong in clean, modern, progressive Canada. They did not belong in our little house where life was supposed to be neat and tidy—and predictable.

I also knew why Dad saw a friend in every Jew or Russian or any person who could strum a guitar and sing a Russian folktune, pitched in minor key and mourning a lost homeland.

5
A Lost Family Is Found

THE NORTH wind doth blow,
And we shall have snow,
And what will poor robin do then?
   Poor thing!
He'll sit in a barn,
And keep himself warm,
And hide his head under his wing.
   Poor thing!

SOMETIMES AT suppertime, after a day of serving customers at the store, as he finished drinking his lemon
tea from his saucer—something I didn't like because I
was sure no one else's father did that—Dad would lean back.
He'd say, "Mama, do you remember that Hans Riesen from
Rosental, who gave me a ride back from Sagradowka after I
found your parents and brought them there?"

He'd push the dishes to the center of the table. He was
through with them, so why should he keep them near? Dad
never wasted time eating. Eating was a necessity to stay alive.
It was not a social function. He joked about English ladies
who stuck out a little finger when they held a teacup.

"Riesen?" Mother'd say. "Riesen? No, not a Riesen—a
Penner, wasn't it?"

"That Riesen was in the store today—going to Mulingar.

I thought he was the one—maybe not . . ."

"From Sagradowka to Rosental, it was a Penner, I'm sure." Mother would start clearing the dishes. She knew such details. I knew only that her faraway family never knew when she got married and to whom—until one day, true to his promise to her, Dad went to find them. This is Dad's story.

One day in June 1921, Dad sat on the steps of the windmill at the edge of the village of Rosental. He watched the heavy horse-drawn wagon of one of the richer Mennonites creak down the road. The hind end of the man resembled the fat sacks of meal piled on the wagon—overstuffed. He had brought ten sacks of grain to be ground. Few people brought that much grain anymore. He must have hidden it somewhere to escape the prying eyes, demanding shouts, and threatening swords of the Makhno bands.

As Dad watched him, he felt the anger rising. The man had treated him like a *Laufbengel*, a boy to be ordered around. But Dad needed the business. The frustration of being landless and without an education hurt. There was no future for men like himself in this country, where the prejudice came not only from the outside but also from his own kind.

This man was like the one in his childhood who had asked his father for a boy to work for him for the summer. His father had agreed. For what Dad would earn, his father could send another cow to pasture. Dad spent the whole summer on the estate, becoming more and more aware of class differences. The owner ate roast duck and other good food in the front room, while the workers ate unpeeled potatoes with hot fat poured over them in the back room. Dad never forgot the smell of roast meat drifting in the evening to the back room where he ate. Though the hired help got up at daybreak to begin the day's chores, the work never ended, even after dark.

Now here was another of the same kind—ordering him like a boy, because he wore *Schlorre*. He glanced down at his footwear. No shoes as yet, nothing but these pieces of wood with a strap of leather across each foot. At twenty-four he was a man with a wife and child. His mother, three brothers, and a sister depended on him. He wanted to leave this country where his head bumped the rafters every time he stretched, but he had a job to do first.

As he struggled with his anger, he felt the saliva welling up in his mouth. Warm. Liquid. Potent. He resisted the temptation to swallow and spat hard on the ground. Then he sat on the steps and watched the fine dust absorb the moisture. Before long it was gone. Only a wet spot.

He knew then it was time to go find Mother's parents in the Black Sea area—at least to learn if they were still alive. He had waited long enough. He had made a promise. His brother Peter, released from prison, would look after the mill. He went home to tell Mother he would leave the next day. Afterward they could think about leaving for another country.

The summer sun had been warming the ground for several weeks, making it possible to sleep on the ground if need be. He pulled an old pair of pants over his good ones, donned a Russian-style blouse that hung loose, slipped his feet into his *Schlorre*, and put bread into a knapsack. Mother added some ammonia cookies and a picture of herself to give to her parents. They said good-bye in the privacy of their room where the baby was sleeping. Mother had faith Dad would find her parents. He looked long into the cradle and then at the embroidered wall sampler that said, "*So nimm denn meine Hände and führe mich*" (Take Thou My Hand, O Father, and Lead Thou Me).

"Did you take some money?" I asked as I listened.

"Money? Probably a few coins. Who had money then? We didn't."

Before he left the village, he went to the local government office, now controlled by the Reds, where his Jewish friend worked. He asked for a travel permit to allow him to move about freely in the Kherson district to the south where he planned to begin the search. His friend gave him what he needed, and Dad pinned the paper into his pants pocket and started walking south. He went first to Kronstal, where he had buried his father and the others more than a year earlier.

Many graves had been added since January 1920, so he spent time looking for the small wooden stakes with the familiar names. Like other graves in which several people were buried, those graves had collapsed, making the graveyard look like a giant face deeply pitted by smallpox. He looked for something to shovel additional soil onto the sunken graves but found nothing. After scraping a bit with a broken tree branch, he gave up and tramped on. His inner hurts and the outer wounds in this graveyard would have to wait for healing. He had more important work to do.

By early afternoon he reached the bend in the Dnieper River where small oceangoing ships came inland to take on cargo and where, once again, the local police were checking travel documents. The commissar, whose duty it was to examine each document and stamp it, was called out of the office as Dad reached his desk, so the man told his clerk, "You look after this man." She, thinking her overseer had checked the papers, stamped them without examining them and sent him out. He left without saying a word, grateful for small mercies. At the dock he found a boat to take him on board in exchange for work as it navigated down the Dnieper to Kherson.

Mother had given him general directions concerning where to look for her parents, for she had often made this trip to the estate while she worked at Bethania. The estate on which her parents had been working at the start of the Revolution had been near the point jutting into the Black Sea, so Dad's first stop was Kherson. That was a large city of about sixty to seventy thousand people on the right bank of the river, about fifteen miles before the river opens into the Black

Sea. He spent the first night with a Jewish student he had met on the boat who invited him to his home. Before he left, the young man's mother gave him bread for the day's journey.

The next stage of the journey wasn't quite as simple, for Dad was looking for Garletzky, the site of the *Khutor* (estate), and trying to figure out how to get there. After a morning's walk, he stopped near an inn at Holoprystan, a place where Mother had often stopped while traveling to her parents' home for a summer vacation. The owner, a short, dark Russian with a heavy beard, noticed the stranger sitting outside under the tree, eating his dry bread.

"Where are you going?" he asked.

"Garletzky," replied Dad. "I am looking for some people who lived there before the revolution."

"All gone—not there anymore." The man shook his head as if in remembrance. "Who're you looking for?"

"Franz Janzen."

"Franz Janzen?" The man stopped to think. "Red hair, German-speaking?"

Dad nodded.

"I know him—he's been here. But don't go to the *Khutor*. Nothing there—everything gone—even the fences. When the Makhnovsky came through, they burned everything—houses, barns, sheds—everything. Hard times." He shook his head again as if to make the memory go away.

"But the workers—where did they go?"

The innkeeper looked at him carefully and said nothing for a while. "You might try some of the villages on the other side of the *Khutor*. Terrible times there . . . on the *Khutor* . . . terrible times all over." His face looked pained.

Dad asked him for a drink of water from the well. As he walked away from the inn toward the road, the Russian called out, "Here, take some bread. You'll need it." With thanks, Dad put the dark rye bread into his knapsack and stepped into the afternoon sun to head in the direction the man had suggested. He felt troubled.

Dad met few people as he walked mile after mile into the setting sun. Toward evening he met an elderly woman, hair loose, eyes filmed by cataracts, wandering along the roadside on her way to evening mass. He fell in step beside her, for he too was weary. She told him that her husband had been killed during the war, and her son, her only son, had long ago disappeared. He had wanted the adventures of a soldier. She cried and scolded her lost son for deserting her as she walked with Dad along the dusty road until they came to the church at the village outskirts. She knew well the way to the Christ on the cross in the niche outside the church. Dad stood there with her in front of the dark-haired Jew on the cross, his head resting as if in sleep. The woman bowed her head, her prayers turning to sobs.

Her mood touched him. Everywhere he looked he saw signs of poverty and hardship. Houses had collapsed and fields were not being tilled. Tumbleweed, already dried out, piled up against the fences. An existential loneliness overcame him as he stood with the blind peasant woman. He knew no one. No one knew him.

Once when Dad was telling the story, I asked him, "How did you feel?" He looked at me, almost startled.

"Lonely," he said. "Lonely." He knew he could be killed within the next five minutes by someone who wanted the bread in his knapsack. What was more, he knew that when he returned to Rosental, it would only be more struggle to survive.

Then he too wept, standing there beside the peasant woman, wept and prayed.

The woman returned the way she had come, but he had to go on. His stomach told him it was time to eat that rye bread. He thought of the way it used to be before the revolution—attics filled with rows of dried apples, corn, beans, peas, and blackberries. Between the windows of the house hung strings threaded with red peppers and onions. Big barrels of pickled watermelons and cucumbers and sauerkraut stood ready for winter use in the cellar. There, too, was the barrel of *Kwass*, the ale every Mennonite family found refreshing on a hot day like this. On the table would have been a huge bowl of fried potatoes, slices of ham on a platter, *Pluma moos*, fresh bread, and coffee. He pulled out the rye bread the innkeeper had given him and munched it slowly.

A man driving past on a low wagon pulled by two wasted animals caught up with Dad as he clopped along the dirt road and offered him a ride for a few miles. He too was unable to say where the several hundred people who had lived on the *Khutor* had fled. Some were certainly murdered the night of the assault.

When the driver was about to turn off to drive to a small broken-down farm, he turned to Dad. "Join us for supper . . . not much . . . you look tired."

Dad accepted. As he entered the small clay-brick house smeared on the inside with more clay, the smell of onions, cabbage, and fat hung heavy in the air. The man and his wife welcomed him, recognizing that he was lonely for his own family. The buckwheat porridge and cabbage soup tasted good. He watched the mother feed her young child by chewing the hard bread then pushing the warm cud into the waiting open mouth. The child was a little older than his little Frieda. They urged him to take another glass of tea from the brass samovar standing on the table, looking almost out of place in that poverty-stricken home. They talked, skirting difficult topics. Both husband and wife had lost much during the revolution—a father, a brother, others.

"Stay the night," said the man.

"No, I must go." Dad could make a few miles yet before dark, although his feet were tired. Their offer tempted him, but he turned to leave.

Later that evening he found a haystack in a field and spread a little of the hay beside the mound and lay down, his knapsack under his head, his eyes turned to the stars. How minute the stars seemed from the field. Did a human being look that small to God? The loneliness of the afternoon overcame him again. He was like one of these stars. He could never spot the same tiny star twice. Did God spot the same person twice? If Dad were lost, who would care? Anna, his wife, would. She cared about her lost parents. She would care about him.

A dog with one eye, hairless, tail wagging, came to him and licked his hand. Dad shoved the dog aside roughly. Then suddenly his mother stood over him, smiling as she used to in the old days when his father was alive. She brought him a great bowl of summer borscht with thick cream floating on top. She urged him to eat. When he had finished one bowlful, she appeared with another, and yet another, as if she didn't know the west wind was blowing hard and he had to get up to go to the mill.

He slept until morning, when the cool breezes blowing over him off the Black Sea woke him. He heard dogs barking in the distance, and a cock crowing. A thrush sang boldly in the trees. It was time to move on.

He shook the straw from his pants, ate the last bit of bread in his sack, and began the walk along the shore of the Black Sea toward the point. Today he had to find the Janzens. The sun beat on his head, forcing him to carry his cap. The wind blew off the water, whipping up sharp particles of sand which stung and stabbed like the many-thonged whip of a demented master. The omnipresent Russian thistle caught up with him, pulled ahead, then stopped to taunt him. He trudged along, mile after mile, and never met anyone who looked even slightly familiar.

He looked into every passing face, but only the cautious eyes of Russian peasants returned his stare, their dark eyes set deep in their sockets, unwilling to yield their secrets. When he asked a question, they pushed words at him through blackened teeth but without a smile.

In three villages strung out one after another, he asked shopkeepers on the main road if they knew any Janzens—a red-haired man with a thin, pock-faced and raspy-voiced wife, and many children—living in the area. Heads shook each time. He trudged on. Toward the point the farmyards looked even more neglected. No gardens, rickety fences. A pig and a few chickens scratched barren ground. Little houses with thatched roofs crouched low beneath the few remaining church domes. He saw uncared-for graveyards.

He wanted desperately to turn back to the wife waiting for him in the house by the mill to resume his responsibilities as husband and father. What was he doing here in this god-forsaken place? Why had he consented to come on this impossible mission? Was this his responsibility as son-in-law? Couldn't his father-in-law look after himself?

Toward evening, as the sun was setting, he came to Proghnow. The village looked no different from any of the others he had passed, with its rows of thatched, mud-daubed huts, struggling flower beds, and fenced-in yards. Whom could he ask about the Janzens this time? No inn. Nothing looked like a store or public place. He was about to knock on the nearest door when he saw a young girl of about ten or eleven, with red braids flying, dart between two buildings at the far end of the street. Something clicked. Red hair like his wife's! He ran, calling out in Low German, "Is your name Janzen?"

The girl paused momentarily and looked at him. Then she turned and fled as if she had seen a ghost. Dad ran after her until he was standing at the door of a broken-down hut into which she had disappeared. Part of the thatched roof was gone, and the mud walls were melting into the ground from the rains. He knocked gently. A tired, dark-haired woman, thin, with pock marks on her face, opened it cautiously. "Are you the Franz Janzens?" he asked in Low German. The woman looked at him. Dad knew that by now he probably looked like any Russian peasant, yet he hoped his words might get the response he wanted. She waited a moment, looked at him again, as if trying to recognize him, then said, "Yes." But the word was a question.

"I'm looking for the Franz Janzens who used to live at Trubetskoye many years ago. I am the husband of your daughter Anna." He unpinned his pocket to produce the picture of Mother. The red-haired girl he had seen on the street stood behind her mother watching. Some other young girls dressed in coarse gunny sacks with holes cut for armholes moved closer to the door. Straw lay on the floor for bedding. He saw little furniture.

The woman spoke, her voice low and scratchy. "Truda came home saying a man had talked to her in the language we talk." She took the envelope, opened it, and looked long and hard at the picture, then turned to Dad, unbelief written in every line of her face. "Is my daughter still alive?" she cried out. Her tears flowed.

In a short while, her husband walked in, having finished his work for the day at a nearby mill. Once again Dad explained who he was, where he had come from, and why. His wife, their daughter Anna, was concerned about them. He had come on her behalf. After a while Janzen's son Franz, about fifteen, came home and Dad repeated the same words.

Like the brothers of the biblical Joseph, they couldn't hear the good news enough. Anna was alive. Anna wanted them to come back. Anna, the short one with red hair, the determined one who knew her own mind, the one who brought them presents when she visited. Anna was thinking of them. She had sent her husband, this strong, self-assured young man who knew what he was about, to help them.

Someone had come to rescue them from this prison of poverty.

After some time the mother sent a child next door with a pail of dried manure to get some fire. Supper, even if meager, had to be cooked for their guest. They ate a simple supper of porridge and hard bread. Dad thought the food at the Russian peasant's place on the way here had been better and more plentiful. The woman apologized for the food, but it was all they had.

Dad looked around. Six children and two adults were living in this squalid shack on the meager earnings of Franz, the father, and his son Franz junior, but it wasn't nearly enough to keep them fed well. They had managed to save one cow from the *Khutor*. When the bandits rushed into their home, they had lined the family against the wall, even the youngest. A sudden scuffle had knocked the gun out of one ruffian's hand and blown out the lamp. The family had fled into the darkness. The buildings had all been razed. They had been here for over two years, and each week conditions grew worse.

"You can't stay here," Dad told them. They knew that. "You'll die of starvation."

Father Janzen agreed. Starvation or exposure would take them the next winter, but he didn't know how to get the family away from this hidden spot back to the Mennonite settlements to the north. The little money he earned was never enough for food, let alone travel permits and travel expenses.

They talked a long time that night before each one found a spot on the straw, which did little to soften the hardness of the dirt floor. By morning Dad knew what he had to do. He had slept little that night. He couldn't leave the Janzen family here at Proghnow. He had found them, but finding them wasn't enough. They had to be helped out of their situation. Apparently there was no one to do it but himself.

"Did they get away from that place?" I'd ask Dad when

he quit talking and was getting ready to go to bed. For him the story had ended. Mother's parents had been found. "Yah, sure. I got 'em out. They went back to Sagradowka."

He wanted no praise. That was my father, the one for whom I was embarrassed when he saucered his tea or spoke with the unlearned speech of an immigrant and not the careful way we were learning to speak English in school; the one who wasn't always most tactful, blundering in because his practical mind found little room for anything that didn't meet practical human needs. He was the one who sometimes made fun of the poems we learned at school or the classical music we wanted to listen to more because it was the thing to do than because we enjoyed it so much. My immigrant father was the one who had risked his life to save a lost family.

For years while growing up, I had a recurring dream that woke me with a terror I could not shake. I would clutch the bed covers for warmth while cold sweat covered my body. The sequence was always the same. Our family, all of us, were fleeing in the dead of night in a decrepit ladder wagon, horses stumbling along in the darkness. Each person clutched a few belongings. I sat at the back of the wagon, feet dangling over the edge, sprinkling the road with my tears, for I was leaving my home and I didn't know when I would be coming back.

6

The Across-the-River Church

MARY HAD a little lamb,
Its fleece was white as snow,
And everywhere that Mary went,
The lamb was sure to go.

"Why does the lamb love Mary so?"
The eager children cry.
"Why, Mary loves the lamb, you know."
The teacher did reply.

SUMMER HAD COME, and it was time to figure out once again whether I was saved. I only faced this question when summer arrived with its clear, blue skies and temperatures warm enough to melt the snowdrifts on the fields and the thick ice on the river. When summer came, we went to the Mennonite church across the river, and dozens of zealous young vacation Bible school teachers from across the river came to our side to make sure we were saved.

I couldn't figure out my discomfort.

Across the river we sang boldly, "Are you saved, washed in the blood?" and other solid gospel hymns. On this side of the river, at the United Church in Blaine Lake, we sang "Jesus loves me, this I know," and the tiny choir sang anthems, an entirely different genre. How can you compare the slow, agonizing "In the hour of pain and anguish, in the hour when death draws near, suffer not my soul to languish, suffer not my soul to fear" with the triumphant "Up from the grave he arose, with a mighty triumph o'er his foes"? In Blaine Lake, a soloist gulped great noisy breaths between phrases. I waited for them.

The music wasn't the real problem. To be saved I had to be sinful and feel sinful. I didn't. I felt good. In fact, I was having a good time and couldn't match my feelings with the conflict-packed stories of conversions I heard over there—stories of days and nights crying on the barn floor under conviction of sin.

To be sure I argued with Annie if she pulled my half of the comforter in bed over to her side, and with Frieda if she tried bossing me around, making me do dishes when I'd already had my turn. I fought with Jakie. He was always getting into my things. I snitched candy, especially maple sugar cakes, when I was in the store. I took it from the boxes at the back of the counter, where I wasn't seen. I ate too much. I hated being poor, even our kind of poor, which was poorer than most but not as poor as the honey-wagon driver or the Metis half-breeds living at the edge of town. Sometimes I flirted, but that seemed natural, not sinful. I didn't drink, smoke, or dance—the truly big sins across the river. I didn't feel sinful. Where could I get that sinful feeling needed for across-the-river salvation?

In the early years when weekly street meetings were held by people from across the river in our village (renowned for its paganism, especially its drinking and dancing) I rushed to the bank corner as soon as I heard the tambourines clatter. Salvation Army people came regularly, in their navy blue-and-red uniforms. The men played brass instruments and the women, in their hard bonnets with big bows tied under their chins, banged tambourines. I always managed to push my way through to the front row, whether my hair was already in rags or not. I was sometimes called by the band leader to sing before the crowd, which embarrassed my sisters no end. But the band leader liked me singing my heart out in the front row. I knew it by the way he smiled at me. He wanted everyone to see such exuberance about holy things.

One Christmas Eve I went to sleep uneasy. Somewhere I had heard amidst the adult chatter that the world would end this night. I knew I wasn't ready. Huddled under the covers, I debated what to do. Annie was sleeping soundly beside me. Her spiritual state was no different from mine, I was sure. I tried to stay awake. I tiptoed to the window. The street was still there. My parents were breathing heavily in the next room. I went to sleep.

One summer, under the steady pressure of invitations to be saved at VBS, the across-the-river Sunday school and revival meetings, I rushed upstairs to the closet and buried my face in Mother's nightgown. I prayed earnestly, "Jesus, come into my heart; Jesus, come into my heart." Then I waited for the outpouring of rich satisfying feelings of salvation, like when the ferry arrived at our side of the river just when we got there and the whole family shouted for joy. But nothing happened. Somewhere I had missed a step in the directions. Mother's comforting smell reached out to me from her gown.

Revival meetings were common those days. Mother and Dad were loyal attenders, concerned about getting us children all into the kingdom of God. At one service Annie and I went forward at the evangelist's repeated invitation. We knelt at the front bench and were expected to pray, but I knew only my childhood memorized prayers. When we came home, Mother and Dad kissed us and wished us well in our Christian walk. Such an open show of emotion was unusual in our family. But again nothing fell into place.

For Frieda, however, something survived after an altar-call response. Concerned about her siblings' spiritual welfare, she read to us every night from Bunyan's *Pilgrim's Progress*. We joined wholeheartedly in her enthusiasm for spiritual things and agreed to look up all the biblical references in the footnotes. But that practice didn't last long, especially some nights when a single page had five or six references. Stumbling through King James terminology didn't increase our Bible knowledge or our understanding of Christian's struggle to reach the Celestial City. We agreed to let him struggle alone. We returned to continued adventure stories that Frieda made up—much more fun.

The news had spread that Annie and I had gone forward at a revival service, so the next time the most regular of our across-the-river VBS teachers saw me, he said, "Sister Funk, how are you getting along with the Lord?" Sister Funk? I was just a child. Getting along with the Lord? I almost looked behind me to see if I had someone tagging alongside me on a leash.

The ice in the river had broken a few weeks earlier. One evening we had driven to the river to watch the massive chunks of ice pushing against one another as they heaved themselves down the waterway, each one determined to get there first. But now the river was ice free and the ferry was operating. Tomorrow we would go back to church across the river.

Saturday was preparation day. My parents believed strongly in the commandment that six days shalt thou do all thy work, and the seventh is the Sabbath of the Lord thy God. There was no doubt about it. Certain work was done on Saturday so we could face Sunday and look our Maker in the eye without flinching. There was housecleaning, baking and cooking, washing hair, and bathing.

At noon Dad took the car to the filling station. Mother spent the morning making crumbcake and jellied fruit salad.

We also took along egg sandwiches and cold lemon tea for our lunch after church and probably a cake and other food in case we invited ourselves to someone's place for *Faspa*. Mother refused to take her horde to friends' homes without contributing to the food supply.

I spent part of Saturday polishing shoes, including Dad's, and then all three of us girls had to learn to read the German Sunday school lesson. We moaned and groaned. Our family spoke mostly English at home by then with Mother and Dad still speaking Low German to one another. But on Sundays we all reverted to German for two hours—and High German at that. The custom in Sunday school was to read the Bible text verse by verse before the teacher discussed the lesson. The children in our classes spoke German every day while our worldly tongues were leaving that language far behind in our pursuit of English.

As soon as the reading in class began, I quickly counted down the row to see which verse would be mine. I sighed inwardly if it was a long one, with many big words. I felt humiliated if the teacher jumped around in class, and I read the wrong verse.

Early on Sunday morning we all piled in the car, three in the back seat, one on the lunch box, and one in front with Mother. Driving to church was usually enjoyable, for Dad liked to sing all kinds of songs, even "Little Brown Church in the Wildwood," with us children joining in the "come's" in the refrain. When I was very young, I traveled in my flour-sack petticoat with an empty cornflakes box beside me because I threw up regularly. The family expected it. Cries to stop for carsickness were heeded promptly. Bathroom stops were more difficult, for it wasn't always easy to find a bush not too far into the field. If necessary, the car stopped on a naked strip of roadway and lookouts were appointed to watch for oncoming traffic from both directions. No one ever explained what the crouching girl was to do if a car drove by.

Men and women entered the church building by separate doors. The men had a ritual that never varied. They entered their small front hall, hung their hats on hooks, combed
their hair in front of the tiny mirror, then shook hands with
everyone in the room. When a man was about to sit down in
the pew, he shook hands with four or five men in the short
row if he hadn't done so earlier, then hitched up the pants
they wore only on Sunday before sitting down.

If the local leaders knew a guest was a preacher, the
guest was asked if the Lord had given him a message for the
congregation. As a sign of respect, the guest could decline. A
preacher was always expected to have a sermon tucked up
his sleeve or in his Bible. Dad worked on sermons nearly all
the time and knew about when it was his turn to preach. Little pieces of paper with ideas for illustrations kept falling out
of his Bible or his pockets. Often he'd come home from the
store at noon with a piece of paper and put it into his writing
desk. The desk was kept locked and was off bounds to us
children, except when Mother gave special permission to get
the magnifying glass.

The building was small with one row of pews for the
men, one row for women, and one row for others. A baby
room with a window looking into the sanctuary enabled
women with small children at least to see what was going on.

Services usually had a short introductory sermon and a
long main one with a period of spontaneous prayer between.
For prayer, we turned around and fell to our knees, brushing
the bits of sand and dirt away from under them first. I wasn't
quite sure what we were supposed to do while looking at the
varnished back of the bench, but it was a change of position
and a chance to whisper to a friend. Adults prayed a long
time. Everyone said a loud "Amen" in unison after each
prayer. There was always a choir and an *Ausgangslied* to lead
the worshipers prayerfully back into the work week.

Sunday school came first, so the church was divided into

cubicles with green divider curtains, women in one class, men in another, and children according to their age group. That Sunday school was different from the one at the United Church in Blaine Lake, which we attended in winter. Here parents as well as children attended. In Blaine Lake, often only I or another sister went to the evening service to represent the family. Church across the river was a family affair, which felt good. The green curtains were the same in both places, but church here had added activities we never came across in Blaine Lake.

Here, for example, at *Prüfung*, a closed member session attended only by adults, converts wanting to become members were tested by their elders to ensure they had really had a conversion. Those candidates still waiting to be *prüft* paced the floor near the church steps. We younger children played outside on the church yard. Sometimes we got too noisy, causing a parent to come out and hush us loudly to keep the ruckus down.

Another unfamiliar service was foot washing and communion. The women went downstairs for this because taking off stockings held up by homemade circles of elastic (maybe even canning jar rubbers) or girdle garters might be embarrassing. The women paired off. Each woman took her turn kneeling in front of the other and washing her feet. We children never witnessed this or communion.

Weddings and conferences, however, were open to all. Sometimes a tent was set up for the wedding, and after the service everyone had lunch of zwieback, sausage or cheese, and cookies—but also sugar cubes. When no one was watching us children, the sugar bowl at the children's table was emptied rapidly. Children had to wait to eat—sometimes through two or three settings of adults.

At the across-the-river church, I heard loud preaching in German; many missionary reports; vigorous singing and a jubilant choir; and spontaneous audible prayer, men in carefully modulated tones and women with tears. After church, people visited with one another eagerly, as if they were soul hungry for one another, not like at the United Church where the adults greeted one another courteously.

In the United Church there were few weddings that I can remember and two funerals—those of a minister and the father of a schoolmate. Services were poorly attended except for the Christmas Eve program, which always filled the small auditorium. Each child present received a bag with nuts, candy, and possibly an orange from Santa, and the room filled with laughter and talking. We waited for weeks for this annual event.

Once when the winter was unusually mild, Mother and Dad decided to drive across the river for their Christmas program. At the end of the program, some men distributed Christmas bags to the children, but we five children went home without because they hadn't expected us and every bag had a name on it. That was a point in favor of the Blaine Lake church. Every child present got at least an orange, even the Catholics.

When it came to children's and young people's activities at the United Church, we took part vigorously. As we grew older, we influenced the direction of activities. Annie and I joined Canadian Girls in Training, the nationwide girls' club, and once Annie even preached at a vesper service on "Wist ye not that I must be about my father's business?" I taught Sunday school when I was in high school. No one raised an eyebrow.

The best part of the day across the river was going visiting in the afternoon after we had eaten our lunch, sometimes on the church yard, sometimes in some farmer's field under a tree. Then, we went on to some family for heavy-duty visiting. Mother might have told our chosen hosts after church that we were coming. We were always welcome, because every housewife had baked a huge supply of zwieback, the two-decker rolls, on Saturday. That with coffee and possibly some homemade chokecherry jelly was considered ample. No housewife need get scared out of her senses at the sight of seven extra people trooping in her door. Mother always brought food, often better than what the hosts served. Dad sometimes added to it in his way.

Often, just before it was time to leave on Sunday morning, Dad would say, "Shall I bring something from the store?"

"No, no, I have here—lotsa—no, don't bring."

Dad would tromp off to check the store one last time and be back in five minutes with change for the collection plate for each of us and a full paper sack.

"What have you brought again?"

"Nothing much—a few chocolate bars." Dad loved to give, especially to children who seldom tasted a chocolate bar.

When we arrived at our farm destination, the fun began. Games, exploring the farm, and especially probing our way through the pig tunnels on hands and knees in the straw-stacks. Dangerous? Probably. But what did we care? This sweaty chasing one another in pig tunnels rivaled any kind of fun we had in Blaine Lake. Worn-out, and dirty, we sat down to *Faspa*—after the adults had eaten, of course, but Mother always saved some of the good stuff for us. She didn't believe in children eating last or not getting any of the dessert items.

Once I watched a guest at a relative's home being offered a second piece of chocolate pie. "I really shouldn't," he said as he shoveled the last piece onto his plate. I watched horrified, knowing I wouldn't even get to taste it and the other children wouldn't even know there had been a pie.

After *Faspa* we left for church in the Bennett wagon, a four-mile drive. We children went with our host's children, while their parents rode with our parents. I found myself fascinated by the horses' heavy haunches rising and falling rhythmically all the way to church. The evening service was

often a Christian Endeavor program, sort of like a variety program with songs, recitations (elocution), and a sermon by a
bashful yet eager young man, pleased that God was tapping
him on the shoulder. If you liked someone's singing, you
could ask that person to perform.
Then we went home, but first to the river. All day Dad
kept a watchful eye on the weather. If a cloud appeared in
the sky, we soon headed for home. If the weather remained
clear, we stayed for the evening. Dad hoped he had allowed
enough time to reach the ferry by ten o'clock; after ten he
had to pay a toll. We tried to guess if the ferry would be on
our side. Driving down the hill, Dad honked the horn loudly
to let the ferryman know we were coming, but it didn't always work.

All the side benefits of going to the across-the-river
church didn't settle the matter of whether I was saved or not;
or whether it was something important only to the across-
the-river people. On both sides, people were dealing seriously with serious stuff. Both made claims about truth, about
eternity, about the most fundamental questions of anybody's
existence. The pressure on me grew heavier and more complicated. It was becoming clearer to me that we had Mennonite connections that were deeper than blood, deeper than
church affiliation, almost deeper than belief in God's saving
grace.

On Saturday evenings in Blaine Lake, Main Street was
always filled with people. Its two blocks, bounded by the
train station at one end and the highway leading to the big
city at the other, were the community's main arteries. Daily
we children crossed Main Street to go to school and to the
post office, passing groups of older men who warmed body
and soul on the benches in front of the bank and our store,
talking, cracking sunflower seeds, and watching village life go
by.

We were sent to Main Street's various business establishments to get whatever Mother and Dad needed. It took courage to carry a money deposit for Dad up the steep steps of the bank into its silent, high-ceilinged chambers. It was a small pleasure to take worn-out shoes to the friendly shoemaker. He added our offering to the growing rows behind him that looked for all the world like a dead-shoe cemetery. During the week we went to Main Street only because we had reason to do so.

On Saturday evenings Main Street was different. The rural population joined local residents for an evening of shopping and visiting on its dimly lit streets. Side attractions included the poolroom, the picture show, a restaurant, or the summer street meeting, perhaps even an occasional drunken fistfight. We passed a rite of passage when we made it down Main Street on our own. As long as we stayed on our side of Main Street and within Mother's calling distance, we belonged to her world and the across-the-river world. But Main Street broke the spell. Beyond it and on it lay life—and temptation. Whenever permitted, my friend and I tramped its two-block length looking for excitement, for Main Street on Saturday evening was the best of life, even if it only consisted of a two-cent piece of bubble gum.

Three black children and a blond-haired toddler of three had somehow come down Main Street into our village with their tiny white mother and a stepfather with graying hair and bristling mustache. The first day Jack, Polly, and Jenny attended our school, I rushed home at noon proud to report that two of them would be in my room. The school quickly accepted these strange children—strange not because of their rich, dark brown skins but because of their unusual heritage. They had come from the circus! They had slept under canvas and in trailers, known the thrill of opening night, and seen the eager curiosity of young boys pushing and meddling among the many vans, trucks, and boxes. They had probably tasted cotton candy, which I could only dream about. They already had a past—an interesting one, not the dull, earthbound routine I and the other children of the village knew as our daily lot.

One evening a crowd had gathered around the VBS workers from across the river who were singing with their guitars and preaching. The speaker had prepared a large paper heart, with one side painted black and the other white. He pointed to the black side and said that it portrayed a heart full of sin. Only Jesus could change that black heart to white, the color on the other side. Only Jesus could save.

"Don't you want your black heart washed white as snow?" he asked the group earnestly.

Jack, the young African-American boy, stood up and lifted his hand high. He wanted to be white, he said. The speaker stumbled, trying to explain that he was talking about hearts, not skin.

The next morning the boy's mother, Mrs. Winters, came to Dad's store demanding an explanation. Her son had come home asking her, "Is sin black? Did sin make me and my sister black? Why are we black when everyone else in this town is white? Is the devil black too?"

She had asked her son to explain himself. What had happened on Main Street? "The children in school say I am black because the devil made me black," he told her. "The Sunday school teacher said that sin is black. Now the man at the street meeting showed me a picture of my black heart."

She was upset. She demanded an explanation of Dad. He was on the village council and had given permission to hold the street meeting. What to do? Dad had seen it as an opportunity for evangelism, dear to his own heart. Standing before him was a small, irate woman in her threadbare coat and worn-down shoes; her whole demeanor showed a heaviness not brought on only by this incident. Dad had to prove to her that sin was the color of her son's skin. The street preacher's statements were an insult to the black race, she insisted.

He promised her an answer. The next week Dad spoke with the street evangelist, the same one who had called me Sister Funk. He smiled, stuttered, and smiled, but had to admit he had no proof that sin is black. The next Saturday the street evangelist's paper heart had a red side and a white side. Before the meeting he went to Mrs. Winter and her children and begged their forgiveness. He would never again say that sin is black. Sin is red, according to Isaiah 1:18: "Though your sins be as scarlet, they shall be white as snow." He publicly corrected himself at the next open air meeting.

If adults, especially across-the-river adults who seemed to have more of the answers, didn't know exactly what color sin was or what was supposed to happen when you were saved, how should I? Here was the man who never called a person "brother" or "sister" unless he knew that person had walked down the aisle at a revival meeting; he had to take back his words. What if the entire across-the-river church was wrong about other matters as well and the this-side church was right?

The next winter I wrote a biography of the apostle Peter for the United Church Sunday school and won a New Testament. I decided to side with the this-side group—for now. Maybe someday when I traveled down the road beyond Main Street myself, I would find better answers.

7

The West Wind Is Blowing

WHO HAS seen the wind?
Neither I nor you:
But when the leaves hang trembling
The wind is passing thro'.

—Christina G. Rossetti

---

*A*NY CONVICTION I had that adults had their lives all sorted out and in neat packages was shattered when I discovered that my father was still figuring things out for himself as an adult. And a lot of pieces still didn't fit neatly into a pattern. Sometimes it happened when the wind was blowing steadily from the west; he stood waiting by the kitchen door, listening for the wind to increase. Because then it was time to go . . .

His parents had first lived near the Ural Mountains in Asia, but the poor soil and unproductive farming brought them back first to Osterwick, where Dad was born. Then they went to Rosental, where they bought the mill which his father, a small quiet man with a small beard, operated until the Russian Revolution. Dad and his brothers helped their father with the mill.

A black-and-white drawing of the windmill by my Uncle John (we were always proud of having an artist in our immigrant family—at least one claim to culture) hung on the dining room wall next to the pantry. The humble wooden windmill stood defiantly, blades extended, daring the wind to turn them.

The windmill rested on a large stone-and-concrete foundation. Then came a round framework of heavy timbers which was well tarred for easier sliding, because the entire mill, not just the top section, was turned to keep the vanes facing the wind. A heavy beam, extending from the lower part of the mill and just above the stairs leading into the mill, was used to turn the entire structure when the wind changed.

Dad's father taught his older sons to operate the mill, to sharpen the huge millstone, and especially to outguess the wind, because each wind had its own characteristics. His father filled the wings of the mill with boards, heavy or light, many or few, according to the strength and direction of the wind. This task could be risky too, Dad knew. One miller decided to remove a few sections from the vanes to slow down the mill after the wind freshened suddenly. As one vane came down, he jumped on to loosen the board. But he didn't finish in time. The blades picked up speed and the miller had to make the round trip.

A miller never knew exactly what time a wind would begin, for it started almost imperceptibly. Dad's father showed him how to wet his finger and turn it in the air to feel the wind even before he could see the branches on the fruit trees in the backyard moving. When the wind cooled his finger, it was time to prepare the mill. The west wind would be steady and dependable for several days at a time. Then there'd be no time for carpentry work or for making *Schlorre*. Sometimes then his mother and the younger children would come to the mill in the middle of the afternoon with a basket of fresh-baked bread and watermelon, and the family would eat

Faspa together in the shade of the mill. Competition for business was keen, and the winds in the Ukraine were unpredictable. Dad often heard his father get up at night, as his father had, and go to the mill when he heard the wind stirring.

The wind became Dad's most common sermon topic. I think he was sorting out life problems in his mind as he preached. His text was often John 3:8: "The wind bloweth where it listeth, and thou hearest the sound thereof, but canst not tell whence it cometh, and whither it goeth: so is every one that is born of the Spirit."

He knew his sermon so well he could preach it at a moment's notice. "When I look outside I can't see the wind, but I can see the wind's activity by the waving of branches. I can't see who is born of the Spirit. But I can see the deeds of the Spirit.

"You can never set the time when the west wind will begin. It starts slowly. I wet my finger and turn it in the air to feel the wind even before I see branches moving. When it cools my finger, I know it is time to prepare the mill. The wind will be steady, dependable for several days at a time. So, many people cannot say the exact day of their spiritual birth."

I listened to my father preach, forcefully, earnestly, pounding the pulpit on occasion to make a point, as was common in those days. Would a west wind ever begin blowing in my heart? When had the west wind begun blowing in his heart?

But he wasn't finished. "During the day the south wind blows and turns the mill against the wind, but as soon as it gets dark, the wind stops suddenly. Then I run out and turn the windmill to face the opposite side, and soon wind comes from the opposite direction. If I don't do this quickly, the wind suddenly turns the mill backward and damages the working mechanism. Some Christians are like the changeable south wind.

"The east wind is a stormy wind. It double-crosses you.

When you watch the clouds, one layer moves in one direction and another layer in the opposite direction. So, if some Christians live two different ways, there will be storm, confusion in their lives. When I see clouds crossing over one another, I don't trust the wind. I fear the wind will break my mill, for it might turn suddenly."

Who was he thinking about? Last week he had seen a farmer who had charged groceries for nearly a year go to the other grocery store instead of his. Dad knew what that meant. The man didn't have money to pay his debt and couldn't face him. Dad had been upset when he told us about it at dinnertime.

"The north wind blows long and strong for several weeks, but as the weather gets warmer, it gets weaker. Nothing is worse than good times for a Christian. Warm weather and clear skies stop the strength of the north wind."

Dad believed in salvation, that was clear, but not in formula conversions. That became clearer as gradually his faith story became mine. I grasped with my heart more than my mind why he felt strong allegiance to the church across the river while a part of him always held back when he sensed legalism creep into the church teachings.

At the age of eighteen, he and other young Mennonite men joined the Russian army before they would be conscripted, so they could choose their service and also receive more pay per month.

"I wanted to see the world," Dad said, but he also wanted to work for the Red Cross as an orderly. The young men got the blessing of the elder at a church service. They were advised, "Don't do anything a Mennonite shouldn't do," as they left for Moscow. At the recruiting office, the officials asked Dad if he was a conscientious objector only to keep from killing others or to avoid getting killed himself. Was he hiding behind his CO status? He assured them he was a conscientious objector to war from the bottom of his heart.

As green country boys, they knew nothing about military training and couldn't keep in step. They were unfamiliar with city ways, such as knowing that sidewalks were for pedestrians and streets for vehicles. The policeman blew his whistle and swore at those awkward country bumpkins.

His older brother John had been conscripted earlier and placed in the cavalry, so he asked to be transferred to be close to my father. For a while the two young men were together, Dad a private and John, who had finished high school, at a desk job on Red Cross Transportation Train 195. The train was staffed mostly by Mennonites. Those with education got the better jobs; the less educated like Dad carried the wounded on litters.

When the young and ignorant soldiers were on leave, they often went to the city of Kiev on sightseeing tours. On one tour, Dad and his comrades visited a large but ancient Orthodox Church.

"At the entrance we were greeted by a friendly priest selling holy belts that guaranteed the wearer protection during the war. I bought one, for my belt buckle had fallen off, but the new one broke almost immediately. My friends thought this was a great joke. However, as we toured the church and were taken past the stations of the cross, I noticed that my Russian buddies kissed the cross and left an offering. I didn't. What they did was just as foolish as my buying the holy belt."

Later they were led through catacombs by monks carrying candles. They were shown mummies, supposed to be very ancient. Dad, curious as always, poked one and discovered it was filled with straw.

His work at the war front was hard, and he was unaccustomed to caring for sick and dying men. On Christmas Eve, 1914, his first year in the army, his unit was stationed at Fort Dubno on the eastern front. That day the officers received the command to move the train to a spur line until further orders arrived.

For a short while time stood still that Christmas Eve as the soldiers waited for morning and what it might bring. Dad pondered to himself, *Where am I? What am I doing here, far from home?* The old freight train had been hastily converted into a makeshift hospital on wheels. The twelve neatly made beds in each boxcar were still unoccupied, for they hadn't reached their destination—the war zone—as yet.

"I was young, inexperienced in life and in taking care of the sick. I knew that when the train filled with wounded soldiers, I would be expected to nurse and comfort the men on the return trip to the Kiev hospitals. . . . And I didn't know how."

As the men in the hospital train on the siding waited for the action to begin, tense yet eager to move on, they watched military trains rush by to the front. Train after train, car after car, loaded with bright young men, roared by. Young and with everything to live for, the men were being transported to the front like cattle to the slaughter.

The early war memories were etched in his mind as if the slaughter had happened yesterday. The outgoing soldiers stared out the windows at the passing scenery. A few waved to the orderlies in the Red Cross train, who waved back. The movement was almost mechanical. Few soldiers talked or cheered. Even in Dad's train, the atmosphere was burdened by silence as the men listened to the dull roar of cannons in the distance.

Without warning a passing train threw a bag of mail to them. At once the train became alive with shouting, singing, and backslapping, as the men from all cars gathered around the canvas bag. Letters. Parcels from home. The men laughed. Then they cried. It was Christmas Eve.

As the letters and packages were opened, memories of the warmth and love of family circles overwhelmed the young soldiers. "All I wanted then was to be back home celebrating Christmas with my family," said Dad.

A young soldier rushed out into the snowy night and brought back a scraggly little pine tree. He shoved it into an old boot to make it stand upright. The soldiers looked at the sad little unadorned Christmas tree; again tears flowed. They ached to sing the old familiar carols but had been forbidden to use German, their mother tongue, because it was the language of the enemy. However, from a corner the soft tones of a mouth organ playing "*Stille Nacht*" brought quietness to their hearts. For a short while, it seemed like peace on earth.

Their peace was rudely shattered by a loud command to get ready to move. The Christmas tree was thrown out the door, the letters replaced in their envelopes, and the mouth organ silenced. The train rolled from its place on the siding to the main track toward the front.

Dad was apprehensive. What would they find there? How many wounded? How many dead? How many sweethearts, wives, and parents would never hear nor see loved ones again? Would he able to endure it?

When they reached the smoking, ravaged town of Brodi on the Austrian broder, scenes of horror faced them on all sides. Few buildings were standing. People cowered in cellars and craters made by the bombs. Even an old cemetery had spewed up decaying coffins. Close by they saw massive fresh graves carefully covered with pine tree branches. Under the ground were buried the bodies of hundreds of brave young men.

But the time for fear and wondering had passed. Their work had begun. An endless stream of soldiers with haunted faces and ugly gaping wounds waited their turn to be loaded onto the hospital train. The orderlies worked steadily until every bed, every chair, and every corner of the train was filled. Then the train began the return journey to the Kiev hospitals. In Dad's car the peace and quiet of a few hours before turned into screams and moans of pain.

The train stopped briefly at a little hamlet. Terrified faces peered into the open doors of the former freight cars. One woman, prematurely aged, face gray and wrinkled beneath her heavy shawl, tugged at Dad's sleeve. "Soldier, have you come from the front?"

Dad nodded.

Her hand clutched his arm more securely. "Did you see my son?" She pulled a picture of a young boy of about fifteen from the front of her blouse.

Dad examined the picture of the young boy in a soldier's uniform several sizes too large, his army number written across the bottom. He looked into the mother's anxious eyes that were trying to force him to say yes. How many times had she asked this question? How many more times would she ask it? Would she ever receive the answer she wanted to hear?

Dad lifted her hand gently from his arm as he shook his head. He turned to answer the call of a sick soldier. He could not face the mother. Christmas Day 1914. For her, for the sick man, for himself, there was no peace.

After several months of working each day with sick and dying men, he was physically weary and emotionally exhausted. About a year after he had joined the army, he applied for furlough and went home to rest. Almost at once he realized that was a mistake, for he was immediately conscripted and ordered to report to the recruiting office at Ekaterinoslav, where he was placed in a Red Cross unit without Mennonites. That unit operated a hospital, a kitchen, a disinfection unit, and a place for wounded soldiers to rest temporarily. As they arrived, they were bathed, fed, disinfected, and after a few days sent to other hospitals according to their injuries. Dad was placed in charge of the kitchen and the feeding of several thousand soldiers a day.

While working at this field hospital, he asked for permission to sleep in an unused room because the barracks were infested with bedbugs. Those in charge neglected to tell him that the room had been used for typhus patients.

"Before long I was sick and placed in isolation. I don't remember what happened, but the nurses told me I had high fever, long spells of delirium, extreme prostration, and a red rash all over my body.

"Several weeks later as I lay in bed one morning, I felt a fresh breeze blowing over me from the open window and looked around. I couldn't recognize where I was. 'Where am I?' " I asked a nurse.

" 'In the hospital,' she told me."

She said he had been very sick and had lost so much weight (he usually weighed about 165 pounds on his six-foot frame) that she had carried him like a child to the next bed to make his bed. When he thought he had recovered fully, the typhus recurred and again he was very ill with a high temperature. A second time he recovered, but the nurse told him, "Soldier, you were a sick man. This time it was close. We nearly lost you."

As he lay in bed watching nurses, orderlies, and doctors flitting by, he knew another wind was stirring inside him, but he couldn't identify it the way he could identify the winds when he operated his father's windmill. *If I had died, what would have happened to me?* he asked himself. He didn't know. He wasn't baptized, and he had no Bible. He felt lost. He had grown up in the *Kirchliche* church where attendance had always been only an adult affair. Children were taught their catechism in school. Before he quit school as a young boy, he had had to learn the answer to the question, "What will happen to your soul when you die?" Yet as he reflected on the story of Lazarus in the bosom of Abraham and the rich man in Hades, he couldn't find the comfort he sought.

Furthermore, he had never been baptized, but that hadn't bothered him before. Time enough for that when he thought about getting married. You couldn't get married without being baptized first. He had never gone to church often, so he didn't know the chorales that the congregation sang without hymnbooks—only with a *Vorsaenger*. His father had led the singing for a time. In their family they had morning and evening devotions, using the *Abriss-Kalendar*, a daily calendar, from which his father tore off the small page of reading material each day. But none of that had ever appealed to him. He had listened only because he had to.

During his illness he had almost died. Someday he would die, maybe soon if the enemy bombed the field hospital. He had to do something about his soul. His friends often asked him about his health, but no one asked him about his inner being, which was rubbed raw with doubt and fear.

One day he saw a Russian soldier striding down the path between the barracks with a big black Bible under his arm. He recognized him as a *Stundist*, so called because they had specific hours for Bible study and prayer. He also knew they loved to walk around with their Bibles for all to recognize them. Maybe this soldier could help him.

"May I go with you to your meeting?"

"Sure, come along."

But the meeting was a disappointment, for the fifteen to twenty persons who had gathered in a small outbuilding sang and prayed together and testified about experiences he hadn't had and couldn't understand. He didn't know their songs any better than the chorales.

He kept on the lookout for persons who might help him. One evening as he walked to the barracks from the field kitchen, he met a conscripted monk who had been friendly to him from time to time, especially after he had become sick the first time. As a religious man he should have some answers, even though some of his kind pulled tricks like selling holy belts that fell apart the first time they were buckled.

"How can I get rid of my guilt?"

The Russian Orthodox monk told him to go and confess his sins.

"Where shall I go?"

"What religion do you belong to?"

"Well, none as yet—I haven't been baptized."

"Find yourself a church leader and confess to him."

On his next furlough, he knew what he had to do to gain peace of mind about life after death. After greeting his parents and brothers and sister, he walked down the tree-lined main road of Rosental to the house of the elder of the Flemish Mennonite congregation. He didn't know what to expect. All he knew was that he had to confess to that church leader.

After the elder's wife let him in, he stood before the older man in the *grote Stoav* (living room), cap in hand, and told the elder he wanted to confess his sins and receive forgiveness because the Orthodox monk had told him this was the way to salvation. He blurted out his biggest sins, as he saw them, one after another as quickly as possible. Then he stopped, waiting for words of absolution.

The surprised elder shook him roughly, "Jasch, have you gone crazy in the army? Why are you doing this? Catholics and Orthodox confess to priests, not Mennonites." Dad backed out of the house, his burden as heavy as ever and the winds of the Spirit still blowing strong.

The next day as he sat on the bench beside the mill, he turned to the New Testament to read the story of the publican Zaccheus and Jesus. The little man in the tree had found peace by making restitution. He would make things right where he had done wrong.

That evening he told his parents about food he had taken from the kitchen window while it was cooling, and the time he had broken a harness strap and let his brother be blamed. His parents responded, "All children do such things. It's all right, Jasch." They saw that he was unhappy.

He went to the teacher, the one who had made life miserable for him as a child because he wouldn't write with his right hand. He tried to apologize for resulting stubbornness and bad temper. He knew he sounded like a bumbling fool, but he made it through his speech.

The teacher, sitting in a dignified manner behind his desk, asked calmly, "Have you learned to write with your right hand?"

Dad had to answer he still favored his left hand.

"Then why are you here? Come back when you have changed your stubborn ways." The teacher turned him back out onto the street, where the sun was going down. His spirit felt as if eternal night had come.

But he persisted. He went to the church songleader and several other places to make amends for past misdeeds, but no one understood what he was after. After each rejection he feared the wind of the Spirit might quit blowing before he had dealt with the unrest in his heart.

His furlough over, he returned to the field hospital, more determined than before to find someone who would show him the way to peace. Someone had to have answers. One day, after a service in a Russian Baptist church, an older man sensed the younger man's troubled spirit and showed him John 3:16: "For God so loved the world, that he gave his only begotten Son, that whosoever believeth in him should not perish, but have everlasting life." The answer was so simple—faith in Jesus Christ as his Redeemer. Fear was replaced with trust and hope. He returned to his work as kitchen supervisor with joy.

Because food was scarce, this being the first year of the Russian revolution, bribery was common at all levels of army life. One day the man in charge of the warehouse returned to his home for furlough. He brought back some sacks of flour with which he bribed the officers to give him an unconditional release from the army. The release papers said he had a rupture and was unable to work. So Dad was promoted and placed in charge of the warehouse, a responsible position,

for it meant controlling all supplies at that field hospital.
A Mennonite army friend from his village also returned
from furlough; he brought several pails of honey. One evening Dad helped him deliver the honey to an apartment a
distance away. For his help, the friend promised to give Dad
a little honey. A woman answered their knock.

"Is your husband home?"

"No."

A man in casual civilian dress walked into the room
where they had deposited the honey. The man asked for the
friend's name, rank, and regiment, then for Dad's. As they left
the place, his friend told him not to worry about what had
happened.

Shortly thereafter both men applied for permission to go
on furlough. Applications for leave came before the commission in alphabetical order, so Dad was called in first because
his name came before his friend's. The officer in charge told
him to undress, weighed him, and asked him some questions. Dad's rib cage formation indicated he had had rickets
as a child. As the medical officer examined him, he kept looking at a paper in his hand. Then he asked for Dad's name and
turned to discuss his heart with the other officers. Typhus
sometimes affects the heart. He told Dad to go home to
Rosental until they called him back and handed him his release papers. The army never called him again. He never
knew why. Had it been honey, God's mercy, or circumstances?

Back at Rosental Dad began attending the newly developed Mennonite Brethren church, which was revivalist, instead of the one his parents had always attended. There he
was baptized by immersion. He had no intention of return-
ing to the elder who had no answers to spiritual need.

Dad also became acquainted with the young people of
the Evangelical Mennonite Alliance Church in Rosental.
When their elder invited the young people of the Mennonite

Brethren church to join them in the Lord's Supper, he accepted.

After that matters got murky. The next week the Mennonite Brethren church leader told Dad the church council had forbidden him to continue taking the Lord's Supper with them because he had taken it with unbaptized believers—meaning those who had only been sprinkled. Some people in the Alliance church chose sprinkling as their mode of baptism but Mennonite Brethren, in their zeal to be biblical, were certain the biblical method was immersion.

"Until you promise not to have communion with that group again and ask forgiveness of the *Bruderschaft* (brotherhood), you can't come near the Lord's table." Dad had left one church to join another, only to be ousted from that one before he had really become part of it. He admitted to breaking one of their rules, but he had done so without malice. He asked forgiveness and was reinstated in their good graces.

But by then Dad had met Mother and they were married in the Alliance church, where she was a member. Shortly after the wedding, the now familiar group of serious-looking men from the Mennonite Brethren church again walked up the lane to the Funk house, where Dad and Mother were living with his widowed mother and family. By decision of the *Bruderschaft*, Dad had been excommunicated from the church because he had married outside the church. He felt almost as perplexed as when he was looking for the way of salvation for his soul. This being kicked from one group to another was confusing.

He couldn't say he was sorry he had married Mother, whom he loved and who was a born-again believer, so he accepted their ultimatum. He rejected their proposal that she join the Mennonite Brethren, which would automatically reinstate him because she had been baptized by immersion. Church affairs seemed to fall into the category of either loveless power or powerless love. "Such a rule is a joke," he commented about this and much else he couldn't fathom about the way the winds blew in the ecclesiastical world.

Mother and Dad both joined the Alliance Church, where he was elected to an evangelistic and deacon ministry and later ordained. Within him grew a hunger for spiritual truth, which he didn't find in the increasing traditionalism of the church to which his family had belonged, a centuries-old church dating back to the Anabaptist movement of 1525 in Europe. Moreover, he longed to be accepted for who he was, not for who he was not.

I knew this long story well, but always I sensed a missing link. One day I thought I knew what it was and that it related to my own perplexity about the churches we attended. A Russian Baptist had helped Dad find salvation. That was probably why he had such a warm spot for Russian Baptists. We never attended the kind of Mennonite churches Dad's Mother and other relatives attended because the elder who turned him away without help had some vague connection to that church. Anyway, the people from those churches were reticent about their faith. They didn't pray openly. They sprinkled their baptismal candidates.

Though we lived in Blaine Lake, in summer, we went across the river to attend a Mennonite Brethren church with which Dad was never quite comfortable, as if the Mennonite Brethren imprint had become smudged in one corner. They had once excommunicated him for marrying Mother who was a believer just like he was. If Dad had been excommunicated from the Mennonite Brethren church, how had he and Mother become members? Why were we attending there? Did he finally apologize for having married Mother?

One day I asked him. I was still trying to sort out churches and being saved and such things.

"When we immigrated to Canada, most people didn't have letters of church membership. All documents were destroyed during the Revolution. There was no Evangelical Mennonite Alliance church here in the area. No one asked questions, so we joined the Mennonite Brethren church in Laird. What did it matter what had happened in Russia?"

What did it matter? I would never find out until much later.

Dad sometimes saw church as a game of "May I?" "Dear elder, may I find salvation?" "Yes, but only if you do it my way." That had been a rebuff he found hard to accept.

Much later, when I was adult, Dad wrote to me, "If you go against the wind, you'll get all the dust and sand in your eyes, but if you go with the wind, you won't. I found that out in my life. Watch out for orthodox members. They can be very brutal and hard; they are ready to stone anyone who rocks the boat of tradition." Where had grace and love been misplaced? Why wasn't it where it belonged—in daily life?

So Mennonite Brethren is what Mother and Dad became in Canada. An expediency. Mennonite Brethren was what I was becoming. Unwillingly at the moment. The west wind had not yet swept over me. I was waiting.

8

The Storekeeper

JACK BE nimble,
Jack be quick.
Jack jump over the candlestick.

MOTHER WAS EMPTYING the heavy aluminum roaster in preparation for the turkey she was going to roast for Christmas dinner the next day. She threw a large pork rind into the mammoth potbellied heater in the front room. At once the rind burst into flames that shot up the pipes to the chimney. We could hear the fire roaring through the red-hot pipes. Mother stood helpless, not knowing what to do.

"Jakie, get Dad!" she shouted to my brother. The store was a short half-block down the street. Jakie whisked out the doorway.

Within minutes Jakie was back. Dad was busy—lots of customers in the store—and he was alone. His clerk had gone on a delivery. He'd come as soon as he could.

Meanwhile, the flames continued to shoot out the chimney toward the dark star-studded sky. Mother stood there panic-stricken. A bootlegger neighbor, slightly inebriated, saw the flames. He pushed open the kitchen door, surveyed the situation, and asked for a sack of salt. He poured it on the fire, watched the flames die down, and staggered out, muttering to himself. Mother continued Christmas preparations.

Later Dad sent a bystander in the store home to find out how the fire was doing. Mother sent back word the fire was under control. Dad kept serving customers. The store had won.

Storekeeping was Dad's life—and became both his mistress and his slavemaster. It provided work, companionship, information, opportunity to encourage and be encouraged, to philosophize, and to politick. He loved it.

He could never allow himself to take time off, especially if the store was open when he was gone. In forty years he never took a holiday that lasted several days. Each morning early, before we were awake, Dad put on a clean apron or smock and left for the store to open it for the early morning trade and get ready for the day's business. Mother laid out his clothes and aprons or smocks as she did ours. Clothes meant little to him. Mother had to push him to buy himself pants or to take off his soiled aprons.

At the store, he stoked the furnace and cleaned out the ashes in winter; brought up the farm produce (like butter and eggs) from the basement, set out the fresh vegetables (lettuce and celery) and fruit (oranges, apples, and bananas), and made a grocery order for the truck driver to take to the city.

When business was brisk, he worked hard. He also expected others to work hard. He couldn't abide laziness—no standing around with your hands in your pockets. When I was on store duty, he expected me to move quickly and look busy by dusting and moving cans to the front of shelves so the store would look full. The front sidewalk of the store, where the non-customers sat by the hour (a carryover from Russia) soon was littered with sunflower husks. Chewing sunflower seeds was an acquired skill. You popped one inside your mouth on one side, cracked it, blew out the husk on the other side, and at the same time popped another seed into your mouth in a smooth coordinated motion. The sidewalk had to be swept periodically.

When business was slow, as it often was in winter, that same group of men gathered around the register in the middle of the store to evaluate their world. The store was also the conduit through which the good and unpleasant events of the entire community filtered through Dad to the rest of the family.

We received day-by-day accounts of finished events, of breaking news, and of continuing stories like that of the sewing machine agent who fell in love with his neighbor's daughter and met her secretly behind Dad's warehouse. Dad sometimes came upon them smooching when he took out the trash. The girl's father wouldn't let the young man into the house because the young man wasn't Catholic. One day the young man came to Dad. "I need money," he said. Dad knew he wanted it for gambling, yet he gave him some money and held the family gold watch as security.

One day in desperation, the young man asked Dad, "How can I get her father to like me? Would it help to become a Catholic?"

"You'd make some Catholic," was Dad's cryptic comment.

"What if I went to confession? Would he like me then? What do I do at confession?"

"Just say you were a bad guy."

The next Sunday the young man tried out mass. On Monday he was back in the store to report he had carefully parrotted everything the other worshipers had done. "But why do they have water in the collection box?" He had put five cents into the holy water on his way out. Finally he quit trying, redeemed his watch, and returned to Manitoba. People who owed the man money for machines he had sold them brought it to Dad to send to him.

Then there was John "Vanilla" Popoff, a young man addicted to drinking vanilla for its alcohol content. Dad recognized Vanilla Popoff's weakness, so he emptied the vanilla shelf, just behind the counter, when he saw the young man coming. Seeing no vanilla in stock, the young man would head for the next store, where the owner kept his supply under the front counter. One day John asked for a bottle. Mr. Lubin reached under and handed him a bottle. John hurried to the outhouse to drink it. In a few minutes he was back, sputtering and fuming, his mouth, chin, and shirtfront splattered a bright cherry red. Lubin had given him food coloring instead of vanilla.

Life was not always fair but sometimes there were advocates of those unjustly treated. A young immigrant woman was elated to be asked to help a farmwife clean chickens for canning. At the end of the long day's work, the farmwife paid her with a pailful of chicken heads. Unable to speak clearly to object, the young woman cried her way home. On the way she ran into another woman who led her back to the farmwife and made the farmwife add a chicken to the pail of heads.

One Saturday evening Dad watched a poorly clothed woman going from person to person collecting money for a family that had lost everything in a recent fire. The Salvation Army, sounding forth at the bank corner at their usual street meeting, donated a little of their small collection, but few others assisted her cause. Then, from his window, Dad saw the town drunk listen to her tale. With tears streaming down his cheeks, the drunk emptied his pockets of their few coins into her handkerchief.

Events like these plucked at Dad's heartstrings for he felt for the human condition. He had struggled for dignity, justice, and equal opportunity all his life. Once, in Russia, his older brother John had made two sketches of the same scene for an art class. Another student offered him 35 kopeks for one. He submitted John's drawing as his own effort to the teacher and received higher marks than John did for his. John had complained bitterly to his mother. "Life isn't fair," she had replied. Dad's most common piece of advice to me also was "Life isn't fair."

In Russia, Dad had known hunger and sorrow, as well as frustration, bitterness, and despair where he had expected love and consideration. His own response of caring when he saw a need was almost a reflex. He liked to give, but never learned there is a reciprocity between receiving and giving. How often I saw him feel compelled to respond to poverty and hardship. Perplexed, he'd push his face into a frown, trying to decide what to do, waving us away with "*Waacht mo!*" Wait. He'd figure out a way. Sometimes he did. His response of bitterness to legalism and hardheartedness was likewise a reflex.

He was always in the front row when something he could do required doing, but he headed for the very back when the situation took him among formally educated people. In Blaine Lake he felt comfortable with his customers. He became friends with the local senator, a horse trader who had made it to high political circles with little education. It was common for residents of Blaine Lake to speak with an accent and a minimal vocabulary. No one minded. The socially elite women in town called him "Mr. Funk," never Jake, and valued his judgment about groceries. We Funks stayed in Blaine Lake, where the community never doubted his innate ability to lead, electing him village reeve for nine years. Yet because of the early wounds to his spirit, he was never able to become authentically incorporated even into this group because he couldn't receive as well as give.

In time I learned to understand better why he clung to Blaine Lake with its multiethnic population instead of looking for work across the river where people like us lived. It had to do with what had happened in Russia where he had been labeled morally inadequate because he was lefthanded.

I always admired my father's dexterity. If he was painting a big sale sign for some product, like apples by the bushel or flour by the ten-sack lot, and had worked himself into a corner, he simply shifted the brush to his left hand and worked around the wet part. His work never got smudged like mine did because he could use either hand equally well. But he was lefthanded by nature. For him lefthandedness was not an extra advantage, but a severe handicap as great as not having a hand. It represented a childhood of pain and loneliness.

When he was a child, all children were required to write with their right hands. Teachers considered lefthandedness a bad habit—like that of a balky cow who jumped the fence every day to chew the grass beside the road. This bad habit could be excised by the diligent persistence of the teacher. His teacher was persistent. Whenever Dad switched hands in the middle of an assignment, his teacher rapped his knuckles till they first glistened white, then throbbed hot and red by the end of the day.

When that approach didn't work, the teacher placed Dad on the four-seater schoolbench beside an older student who elbowed him sharply in the ribs if their arms clashed on the desk. Sometimes the teacher tied the offending hand behind him; he was certain Dad was only playing stubborn, and a child's stubborn will had to be broken before it ruined him for life. On the playground at recess, he was never chosen for the baseball team because the teacher shouted loudly at him above the children's voices to use his right hand in batting. He was usually left standing on the sidelines, waiting for recess to end.

The pain and humiliation of being regularly punished for what he couldn't seem to change was too much for him. He learned to write with his right hand, but never felt comfortable at school. One morning, long before his eight required years of school were completed, he told his mother he wasn't going back to school ever—and he retreated to a sphere of life where his handicap would not be as apparent.

For a time that meant being his mother's helper at home, running errands and helping with laundry and garden. Dad hated that as much as writing with his right hand. Not a boy's job. His mother, an open jolly woman, and one who would stomach no ruckus in her household, hurt for the shame of her second son and protected him, for he had many worthwhile traits. He was curious, bright, venturesome, and sensitive to needs. The two, mother and son, developed a close relationship that lasted until her death in Canada at the age of 84. His brothers complained loudly that the *Malchbraat* was not used on Jasch as much as on them.

As Dad grew taller and stronger, he became his father's helper in the mill that stood at the edge of Rosental. Dad found millwork much more to his liking than making manure cakes for fuel, cleaning the barn, or milking the cow, which was all woman's work. When business was slow, he liked to stand close to the group of men who gathered by the bench outside the mill and listen to them exchange village gossip and opinions on world affairs. Though he didn't get a formal education, he got a broad one and a very informal one.

After school and during summer vacation, he joined the other boys in their fun, like the annual spring snake hunt in the ravine and woods near their village. That was always a great day for the boys and a few of the braver girls. Their only weapons to kill the poisonous snakes, recognized by the diamond on the head, were forked sticks and clubs. The boys had a wonderful chance to show off their prowess and bravery, and each one tallied his spoils at the end of the day. They learned that if you dazed a snake with a blow to the head, you could play crack the whip with it and scare the girls silly. Sometimes they buried the dead snakes in an anthill and came back a few days later to retrieve a perfectly clean skeleton. No one shut Dad out because he was lefthanded.

In winter, Dad joined the boys fishing on the river, which usually froze over soon after Christmas. This sport was somewhat risky, for the ice had to be heavy enough to support the boys, yet thin enough to cut through with an axe. Often the river had large open spaces of flowing water as they skated along together. When they spotted a school of fish near the surface, the boy with the mallet hit the ice hard, stunning several fish, which immediately turned belly-side up. Another boy quickly chopped a hole in the river. The others tossed the fish onto the ice with top speed, for as soon as the fish recovered from the blow, they disappeared into the water again. The stunned fish were tossed into a sack and the procedure repeated at the next sighting. The sack of flopping fish was carried home to be fried for supper.

Sometimes Dad listened to his older brother John and his friends discuss what they had learned at school. Some of these friends were sons of wealthy parents who owned factories and large flour mills in Chortitza, the adjoining city, and had even done some traveling. Dad's father, landless and owner of a small windmill—not a steam-powered one—belonged to the *Anwohner* (landless) class, which bothered his mother. She felt the class difference keenly and passed some of that feeling on to Dad. He felt it even more between his landless group and those below him—the Russian peasants who ranked far beneath any Mennonite—landowner or landless *Anwohner*. He had seen them sleeping in the barn, eating food by themselves in the kitchen (often poorer in quality than what their employers ate), and watched them whipped for insubordination. His intuition told him this was wrong.

Because Dad was not going to school, he had time for a few of his personal projects, like trying to entice the swallows, an omen of good fortune, to build nests in their barn. He worked hours finding ways to make the swift birds feel welcome by building little ridges and shelves for them to perch on. He lay on the grass, watching them dart in and out freely, no one scolding them for using one wing more than the other.

His parents soon noticed that their dropout son Jacob was good in "calculation." He could add up a column of figures faster than anyone else in the family. So when he was about fifteen, instead of hiring him out to a farmer, his father sent him to work as an apprentice clerk for the owner of a general store down at the other end of the long street running through Rosental, with its rows of similar houses on each side.

Only bulk groceries and staples like tea, lump sugar, chicory, bean coffee, salt, yard goods, thread, buttons, wicks, candles, and hardware were sold. Customers brought along containers for syrup or other bulk items. Strings of smoked herring and other products hung from the ceiling. Paint was sold in powder form, with bright orange most popular for wooden floors. Women did their own canning, so no canned goods were offered for sale. They made their own *Prips* (cereal coffee), so not much of that was sold either. When a household needed meat, they asked if someone else needed some too, so a whole carcass was disposed of at once, making a meat market unnecessary.

Dad's young brother Peter visited him in his spacious living quarters at the storeowner's residence and was much impressed at how far his brother had come in life in such a short time. But the apprentice clerk wasn't nearly as impressed, although he liked his employer and his job. The employer also liked his new employee because he was quick and eager to learn and didn't have to be told twice what to do. The employer and his wife asked Dad's parents if they could adopt him, not unusual in Russia where families were often so large that it was difficult for poor parents to provide for all family members. Dad's parents refused the offer. They loved their lefthanded son.

In that store, Dad learned his first lessons in survival as he watched his employer and listened to the daily round of gossip. He heard that if you have a problem with shoplifting or if someone persists in breaking the simple rules of humanity, you take matters into your own hands and make it impossible for those persons to show their faces in society for a long time. The men laughed a long time about the punishment of several thieves.

The fruit in the orchard of a close relative was disappearing during the night. So at dusk, three men waited in the nearby hedge with a muzzle loader, tamped with rock salt. For several nights nothing happened as they waited near the orchard. Then one evening, they heard voices and stealthily tracked them down to find two young men filling sacks with peaches. The watchers sneaked up, and when they were quite close, they blasted the thieves' backsides with salt. The men ran, leaving the fruit behind.

The next day the villagers chuckled to hear that two hired hands from the other end of the village were spending the day sitting in a watering trough to get salt out of their haunches. But they wouldn't tell how it had gotten there.

When business was slow in the store, the young apprentice was used for other work, to his distress. The storeowner's stout wife found pushing her two toddlers in the baby carriage difficult, yet she loved to visit her friends and drink coffee with them in the afternoon. She persuaded her husband to let his fifteen-year-old clerk push the carriage down the main street to her destination and then come back for her in about an hour's time.

The route of the procession led past the schoolyard where the children played outside. The woman strode ahead, while Dad followed far behind with the baby carriage. As soon as the schoolchildren spotted him, Dad was in for it. They teased him loudly the full length of the schoolyard for doing girls' work. He vowed never to push that baby carriage again, but didn't know how to get out of the job.

The next time he was conscripted for women's duty, in his haste to move past the schoolyard as quickly as possible, he wheeled the baby buggy too close to the sidewalk edge and the two toddlers tumbled out, howling worse than the wolves at the edge of a Siberian village in the dead of winter. To their screams their mother added her loud scolding at his clumsiness. She gathered babies and buggy and wheeled it home herself, which suited him just fine. She never asked for his help again.

His job as clerk folded when the store closed, so he moved to the cooperative for another year and a half, and then to a third store for another two years. By then he knew what he wanted to do in life: to be a storekeeper and to own his own store someday. But that didn't happen in Canada for four decades. Until then he was just the manager, working for someone else. And waiting.

9

The Storekeeper's Daughter

GRAY GOOSE and gander,
Waft your wings together,
And carry the good king's daughter
Over the one-strand river.

WE CHILDREN GREW into our turn to help in the store. My turn came after Frieda and Annie and before Susie and Jakie at the tail end of the Depression and during the early war years. In the 1930s business was done mostly with relief vouchers and credit. Few people had cash. One farmer with a large family came to the store every Saturday evening with one dozen eggs to exchange for ten cents, the going rate, so that each of his ten children had one copper to put in the collection plate the next day.

One Saturday it was my turn to put on one of Dad's smocks and head for the store. Most of the years I worked in the store, a big copper cent bought one or two good-sized pieces of candy and a nickel a fairly heavy chocolate bar or an ice cream cone, even a bottle of pop. Groceries were delivered free to the ladies of the community by bicycle or by a little red wagon after they either phoned in their order or walked to the store and gave it to Dad. He stood at the counter and gathered items one by one.

I never liked to answer the phone. I was afraid of it. My heart pounded when it rang if I was in the store alone. I'd pick up the receiver and shout, "OK Economy Store."

But people at the other end didn't want a young female; they wanted my dad. "Yacko, Yacko!" they'd shout. How could I tell them Dad wasn't in the store when they didn't speak English and I didn't speak Russian? How could I interpret their broken English when they tried that language? I prayed always I would not have to use the phone on my shift.

The other challenge was wrapping groceries. They were never piled in sacks but wrapped in paper. Dad taught me how to wrap big piles of assorted cans, small cartons, and bags so the package wouldn't fall apart in the bearer's arms on the way home. I learned to tie the package firmly, wrapping the string around my finger and breaking it with a jerk. Sometimes I developed a gouge in my second finger from the sharp string. After a while I learned to protect it each Saturday with a brown paper tape bandage.

Dad also showed me how to make change. I learned to count from the amount of the order to the amount the customer had given me. I learned to fill shelves—the front always had to look full even if the back was empty. I learned to cut ten-cent wedges of cheese to order. Few customers were willing to pay for a twelve-cent wedge of cheese, because it meant two cents less for something else. Everyone always knew to the penny how much money they had to spend. Some customers didn't think I could cut cheese accurately, but in time my eye judgment became as good as Dad's.

I learned to weigh peanut butter into jars customers brought with them. I could detect if the dairy butter brought in by farm women for us to sell was rancid. Some lady customers opened each pound and nicked a little piece with a fingernail to taste it. We always informed them who had made the butter, if we remembered, and some farm women's butter was more in demand than others.

Farmers sometimes charged grocery bills for a whole year until they sold their harvest in fall. Then they walked in with a big roll of bills, and said with a cheerful defiance, "Jake, how much is it?"

Dad would bring out a fistful of charge slips, add them up on the little adding machine, and deduct a discount for some reason or other. The farmer would hand over the right amount. There'd be a lot of good feeling passed around. The next week the farmer would be back to charging groceries again. The farmer who couldn't pay took his trade to another store and left Dad with a stack of unpaid bills.

We also charged, but in a different way. A part of my world closely tied to the store was our home bookkeeping system into which each child was initiated before he or she was out of diapers. Without realizing it, Dad taught me honesty and pounded into me the importance of paying bills. Though people might not be fair with me, I had to be fair with them by paying my debts. A sturdy piece of cardboard spiked on a nail on the kitchen cupboard was our record book. Everything brought home from the store in cash or products was recorded on that paper.

Dad valued honesty above everything. Villagers respected him for his trustworthiness. They brought paychecks to him to keep so they wouldn't spend the money on drinking or gambling. He wanted to maintain that honesty in his relationships with the store owners, although he had great freedom as manager. When Dad sat down to supper he always asked, "Did you write down what you took from the store today?" If we hadn't written down our transaction, a major inquisition broke out. So I tried to remember: Crayons, five cents; butter, ten; money for shoe repairs, fifteen.

Every Saturday evening I watched fascinated as Dad rapidly added the long crooked row of figures written in many persons' handwriting, catching his breath at the end of each column. Next he deducted his weekly salary, first $15, then $20, and many years later $25. We always owed that sheet of cardboard, especially in fall when taxes, coal for winter, and school fees came due. Winter clothing had to be bought. At times we were two or three weeks' salary in debt to the store for weeks on end. Dad would look grimmer each day when he glanced at the cardboard, which glared down at us like a fire-eating dragon. My September birthday always passed unnoticed. Who had time to celebrate amid canning, harvesting, and major fuel purchases for upcoming cold weather?

Our home always remained modest, but Dad was entranced with the many new gadgets this country offered for sale or trade. In time we owned a large variety of musical instruments. No one could play them, but he hoped some day the right combination of musicians would turn up in his family to return him to the Russia of his boyhood, which meant simple tunes in minor key. Later we owned a player piano that we girls all played vigorously; a polyphone, in time converted to a washstand because no one fully appreciated the tinkly music box sounds it emitted as the giant wheel turned round and round; a hand-cranked gramophone (phonograph); a lantern slide projector powered by a small lamp; and a pump organ, to name a few of the more useful and respectable objects. The hand-cranked movie projector was exchanged for an electric one because if the operator got tired the figures on the screen got even more tired. But at least Dad could select the films for us. "Better than Mickey Mouse," he commented.

Dad also brought home a radio—a monstrous affair made of wood with dozens of shiny silver tubes inside and whirling dials in front. It sat high on a shelf in the dining room; we children were forbidden to touch it. Evenings, Dad adjusted the dials to get a station. The unwilling creature rejected his advances by whooing and wailing with sad tones.

Dad loved to surprise Mother with things he knew she

wanted—new dishes or a replica of the broad-brimmed hat she was wearing when he first met her. He found it hard to show affection with words or touch, so he brought home concrete symbols of his love, although he could ill afford them. Mother accepted each item on its own merits, sometimes grudgingly, sometimes gladly, because they came from Dad. Dad was her husband whom she had promised to love, honor, and obey until death parted them.

I carried home many products Dad had taken in exchange for store debts—butter, berries, cream, fish, and chickens. In better times he threw the fish in the trash because Mother wouldn't clean them and he didn't want to. If he couldn't sell bartered goods, we ate them at home, these and anything that was overripe, dried out, squashed, and dented. I never knew what a firm yellow banana, soft mild cheese, or pink bologna tasted like until I was grown up. Our cheese and bologna always came home rock hard and dark in color. Peanut butter, because it came from the bottom of the 25-pound pail, required a bit and drill to dig it out. But that was the life of the storekeeper's family.

Working in the store was a course in getting along with the customer and the competition. Putting one over on a customer who wanted to put one over on you was an art. One day a farm woman went to the other grocery store with ten pounds of butter. She didn't want to sell it, but would the storekeeper exchange it for another woman's butter? A mouse had fallen in the cream and her family wouldn't eat the butter, though it was good.

"Sure," Dad's competitor replied. He took it down to the basement. He rewrapped her butter with new butter paper and brought it back without saying a word. Life wasn't fair if a mouse fell in the cream, but justice had its own way of settling accounts.

Competition was keen between local stores with a great deal of price cutting; to keep them secret from competitors, prices were seldom advertised. The owner of the other grocery store usually didn't have the nerve to come into Dad's store or to send his wife to find out Dad's prices for flour or butter. But he sent spies and then reduced his own prices, even if he only had one box of prune plums to sell. That forced Dad to lower his price on a whole carload of them, cutting Dad's profits.

If Dad advertised a product in the window, the competitor lowered his price at once. This game had to end, Dad decided. He had bought about seventy-five pounds of butter at a high price and realized he would lose money if he tried to sell it at that price. No one would buy. So he played his competitor's game. Dad asked a friend to take the butter to his competitor and in exchange buy sugar, a more stable commodity, to cut his own losses. The story leaked out, and the competitor found he had bought all of Dad's high-priced butter.

Certainly life wasn't fair, but it helped to learn to live by your wits in a society in which the customer was always right but was still sometimes stealing you poor—and you had pledged to live uprightly. Life hadn't been fair when the teacher expected Dad to write with his right hand. It hadn't been fair when he watched vigorous young men being slaughtered in the war; or when four of his close relatives died in two weeks and he alone buried them; or when he, the son-in-law, went looking for Mother's family when her older brothers and even uncles stayed behind.

I watched Dad deal with people who made life unfair through their dishonesty. Some kinds of stealing were easy to deal with. For example, there was Pete D. with the low-slung pants. At what moment would they would slide to the ground? What secret mechanism kept them up? A cigarette hung from his lower lip, also defying gravity. Unshaven, grimy, mumbling words from the side of his mouth, he gave Dad his order. I hated to serve him, but Dad kept close track of him from the minute he put his foot in the store. When he added up Pete's bill, he added five cents for the bar of soap in his pocket.

Justice was important, but the kind of punishment that worked best in our small community was shame and disgrace. "What will the people say?" controlled our behavior as children. We were reminded of that constantly. We children were not to allow the Funk name to be dragged into the gutter.

A young boy regularly stole chocolate bars from another store owner, so one day the man planned his revenge. The boy backed up to the open counter and slipped a bar into his back pocket, unaware that as he walked out he was pulling along on a long black thread a card reading, "I stole a chocolate bar." The church officials in Hawthorne's *The Scarlet Letter* could have taken lessons from store owners in Blaine Lake.

Little things that could be slipped into a pocket were often taken. One day Dad saw an older, fairly well-to-do man pocket a bar of soap. As the men gathered around the floor furnace for their daily round of conversation, Dad brought up the subject of stealing and told a story about a rich man who stole a bar of soap from a poor man. Before long the man suddenly left. The next day he brought Dad a plucked chicken as a gift.

On Saturday evenings the store remained open until all activity on Main Street had closed down. In summer this took until well after midnight. When the dance in the Palace Theatre ended, the customers returned to the store to pick up their groceries, purchased earlier and left standing against the wall with their name and "paid" or "not paid" crayoned on their box. Some bought additional groceries, depending, I guess, on how much money they had left after the dance and the time spent in the pool hall.

Dad, the clerk, and I rushed around bringing customers

what they wanted—soap, salmon, bread, and sugar. Dad carried out heavy bags of flour on his shoulder. I liked working in the store when business was brisk and when I could handle what fell to me.

Finally the last customer walked out the door. The cuckoo clock on the chimney crowed—it was 12:30 a.m., sometimes closer to one o'clock on Sunday morning. Dad would pull down the wrinkled green blind on the front door, pull his keys from his pocket and lock it, and switch off lights.

Nearly always Dad turned to me at this point, somewhat hesitatingly, brushing his forehead with that sweep of his hand that became more familiar over the years. He would say, "Take a drink, Katie." He always said my name.

I'd walk slowly to the open water cooler where the bottles were kept and reach in, feeling in the dark water for a cold Orange Crush that had escaped someone else's search. The cooler was refilled with bottles all evening. I'd open it against the bottle opener on the side of the cooler, letting the cap fall into the nearly full container while reminding myself to empty it. Then I'd lean against the counter to drink and watch Dad. A soft drink. Once a week. My reward for working. My sisters and brother didn't get one. My feet ached, but I felt a closeness with Dad and the clerk. We had kept up.

Dad and the clerk moved around quickly putting away perishables. Some were carried to the cooler basement. Those that remained on the display shelves were covered with a cloth so the flyspray Dad jerked around in huge sweeps wouldn't fall on them.

Then Dad would hide the day's receipts, for the bank was closed. He distrusted banks for his personal money but he had to use it for the store accounts. Dad was not alone in his fear of being robbed. Women customers sometimes fished money out of underskirts, bloomers, and bosoms; and men wore money belts or pinned their shirtpockets shut. Dad made all personal transactions with cash, frequently carrying around large sums of money.

On one occasion this practice backfired and showed him again the unfairness of life. One winter my sister Annie became seriously ill with appendicitis. By the time Dad and Annie arrived by train at the hospital in Prince Albert, her appendix had ruptured. She had to stay there longer than planned. The bills mounted, but Dad, true to himself, paid the doctor and hospital bills. Years later when the doctor died and his estate was settled, Dad received another bill for the operation. He had kept no receipt and probably had paid in cash, so he paid it again because he had no proof of payment.

I wasn't supposed to be watching when he hid the little cigar box full of money, but I knew that sometimes he placed it behind the boxes of Oxydol on the shelves, sometimes behind the coffee. Tonight he hid it in the cubby hole under the front window display shelf. I knew about this hole but kept my mouth shut. Certain things you never talked about outside the family. Certain things you never talked about.

"Go home, Katie." He'd let me out the door as soon as I had finished my soft drink. To prevent robbery, he was almost religious about securing doors. You locked the door then tried the door at least once, maybe twice. I do that to this day.

Sometime we walked home together, he at his speed, I at mine, sometimes trying to catch up. If I did or didn't was my concern, never his. If I was alone, I'd dash half a block home. Then I'd make a quick trip through the darkness to the outhouse near the alley, ducking around the shadows of the *Banya*, our much-used steam bathhouse which squatted beside the outhouse, like friends in the night. If it was very dark outside, or the weather unfavorable, the garden served as well. Then I went through the dark house upstairs to bed, beside Annie. I knew Mother would be waiting in the double bed which nearly filled my parent's bedroom across the small hall.

"*Bist du das, Katie?*" I'd whisper a brief "Dad's coming," and crawl into bed beside Annie, hoping she wouldn't notice if I pushed my cold feet gently against hers. Next Saturday Dad and I would do it all over again. We were a team.

10
Beyond the Tumbleweeds

WHO HAS seen the wind?
Neither you nor I:
But when the leaves bow down their heads,
The wind is passing by.
—Christina Rosetti

---

*I*F OTHER VILLAGE children heard stories about their immigrant past, they never shared them. Nor did I share mine with them. They were not stories to be retold, only to be stashed away deep inside like unused jewels in a safe deposit box. Dad had great difficulty telling the story of his own imprisonment by the Red army in 1918, after the Bolshevik defeat of the Whites. I think it was because the story reflected badly on his brother Peter. The Reds were rounding up sympathizers and supporters of the White army. When Peter joined the White army, that brought trouble for his father. Next the Reds came for Dad as the brother of a White army sympathizer.

At their headquarters Dad removed everything from his pockets but a small hymnbook, which he hid in his pants. He wanted something with him when he went into prison. Sometimes he hid it under the lining of his boot. The officials would have punished him severely if they had found the hymnbook, because it was written in German.

He was pushed into a small room already overfilled with men and women, all crowding around the one tiny window for light and air. The prisoners were allowed no contact with the outside world. They took turns lying down.

When Dad was led out to be questioned after being in near darkness for days, the sunlight blinded his eyes. A young Jewish girl, a university student, interrogated him.

"What is your name?"

"Jacob Johann Funk."

"What did you do during the war?"

"I was a soldier on the western front for four years— until the armistice."

"What was your rank?"

"Corporal."

"What kind of work did you do?"

"I was a stretcher bearer."

He could see she had his record in front of him. But she asked the questions anyway. She was leading up to the big one.

"You have a brother Peter?"

"Yes."

"He joined the army of the hated Czarists?"

"Yes."

"Why did he do that?"

"I don't know. I told him not to, but he enlisted anyway. I couldn't stop him. I told him he shouldn't go, but he did."

"Where is he now?"

"I don't know. He hasn't come home—maybe he's dead."

"What do you want to do now?"

"Go back to my village, my family."

"Did you have anything to do with the Czarists?"

"No."

"Take him back to prison."

Dad had little hope of release after that interview. Each night the guards came to their prison room, usually in the middle of the night, to wake everyone and call out some names. Those called would get up, say good-bye to their friends, and march out with the guards. Then the others heard shots—and they knew.

In the morning as they crowded around the little window, they could see the guards gather up the bodies and haul them away. Every day those remaining had a little more room. Dad could even lie down. The little hymnbook was a source of comfort and strength. He penciled a few of his own thoughts in it here and there and marked favorite hymns.

Sometimes during the day, the guards came and called out names of people to be released. If they called out names at night, the prisoners were shot. One day, just at daybreak, Dad heard his own name called. Did it mean release or death? He stood up, kissed his friends on both cheeks the way Russians do, wished them Godspeed, and walked through the door. Outside two soldiers with rifles motioned him to walk between them. They marched in step down the hall. Where to, he didn't know. He just followed them. Ahead he could see the wall where people were shot. Would that be his end?

The guards pushed him past the wall toward the gate and opened it. They handed him his passbook. They ordered him to go home. The gate clanged shut. He was free.

Trembling all over, Dad started to walk, expecting to hear them call him back or to feel bullets. Nothing. He was free, really free. The nightmare was over.

He told that story only once to my brother, when he was well into his eighties. He found greater joy in sharing other stories with happier endings with us children. Sometimes just a question inadvertently asked brought a deluge of information.

The story of finding Mother's family which was lost in the revolution always ended with his finding them. But what happened after that? I needed another chapter to complete the story. "Did you ever get the Janzen family back to where they came from?"

Dad had found himself at the small village of Proghnow, near the Black Sea, with a group of strangers whose only link to him was through his wife. The lost family had been found, but not really found until his wife could put her arms around them, one by one. Again he felt frustrated. The injustice of their suffering compelled him to help, but he lacked know-how and money.

"By the next morning I had a plan," he told me, long after the telling of the family getting lost and being found. "I decided to return to the Mennonite district of Sagradowka, where the Janzens had lived originally and where I knew some relatives still lived. Maybe someone there would take the family in until they were able to support themselves."

That seemed the best plan—the only plan. To leave the family in Proghnow meant surrendering them to a slow and painful death by starvation and disease, if the damp harshness of the winter alongside the seashore didn't hasten it.

Once again Dad pulled the old pants over his better ones, took as little food from the family's small supply as possible, and walked back the way he had come. On that trip the wind, the sand, and the runaway thistles were at his back. Young Franz walked with him to keep him company as far as Holoprystan, where he had met the innkeeper. There he sent a postcard to Mother in Rosental, hoping it would reach her.

Next Dad found a way back to Kherson and headed north toward the village of Friedensfeld in the Sagradowka district. Day merged with day as he trudged alone the long distance of fifty to sixty miles. He lost all track of time. Yet he couldn't let either weariness or his longing to return to the house by the mill stop him or change his direction.

He recalled that as a young boy, when the mill was being fixed, he used to crawl up the iron bars on the high chimney, which were actually too far apart for his short legs, to look out the window near the top. Far below lay the farmsteads, steam flourmills, factories, and other buildings. In the distance was the road out of the village that led to freedom. He loved to look and wonder where the winding road led, but always, too soon, his father called him down to safer territory.

At fourteen, when an uncle and family left for America, Dad determined to follow that road to the land of opportunity across the ocean. There was nothing in Russia for a left-handed boy with a grade-three education. He had somehow gotten the papers to leave from the authorities and asked his father to sign them, but his mother refused to let his father sign. The longing to leave behind the land in which families got lost, people went to bed hungry, and government officials imprisoned and sometimes shot people without trial grew stronger in him. When he returned home to Rosental, he would think about leaving.

Toward evening, after passing through several small Mennonite villages, each with its row of almost identical houses on each side of the tree-lined street, Dad came to Friedensfeld. Though it had been Mother's home territory, it was all strange to him. He stopped at the first household and asked the men sitting outside the house on the bench in the evening air about relatives of the Franz Janzens. The men stared at him and at his dusty clothes and worn *Schlorre*. They probed why he had come. Across the street another group of men also stared. He felt like a dancing bear in the zoo.

The men directed Dad to a house down the street where Mother's brother lived. They followed his steps with their eyes. That brother had been working as night watchman on the same estate as the elder Franz Janzen. When Dad located the brother, the man admitted he had feared to return to the area because he had made many enemies of some of the pilfering Russians at the estate. He too had wondered about his parents—but done nothing.

Together they went to the elder Franz Janzen's brother, who had resigned himself to the thought of the whole family having perished long ago. He rejoiced to hear they were still alive. He agreed to help, but he wanted Dad to bring the family to Sagradowka. He himself didn't feel up to it.

That evening, for the first time in about two weeks, Dad slept under a traditional feather comforter and dreamed nothing. But as soon as he awoke, his mind shifted to the family cowering in the mud hut pounded by the strong ocean winds. Among them he saw the waiting face of his wife, my mother. He prayed for strength to go back to Proghnow.

After a night's rest, Dad was on the road again, bread in his knapsack. Kherson was once again his destination. His *Schlorre* slapped a pattern into the dusty road until he reached the port city. There a fisherman who had known the Janzens agreed to ship him aboard his sailboat across the inlet in exchange for work.

"I thought I knew something about the wind because I had operated the mill for my father, but sailing on that boat was a new experience," Dad often told us. The ship was not going with but against wind. The captain was using wind in a way Dad knew nothing about. The two men had a good time discussing the ways of the wind.

At the other shore, a farmer transporting a load of hay was glad for company and invited Dad along. He hopped on readily to avoid the long walk to Proghnow.

When Dad knocked at the door of the mud hut the second time, the Janzen family was overjoyed to see him. Only smiles. No apprehension. They had been waiting every day for him to return with news of relatives they had not seen or heard from in several years. He told them the plan—to return to Friedensfeld to live with relatives temporarily.

"How are we going to get there?"

He didn't know—not yet. To travel by himself hadn't been easy but was possible. To travel with two adults and six children in addition to himself seemed impossible. He had no money and they had no money. The only saleable item was the cow, a half-starved creature, whose ribs poked through scabby skin. She carried the gaunt look of doom. They discussed one travel plan after another and discarded all. All seemed like reaching for the moon.

As they ate their simple meal, Dad remembered that while he was in Friedensfeld he had seen a neighbor woman come into the house to borrow a pinch of salt for the soup she was making. In the inland areas, table salt was in short supply. Salt was the solution to their problem. It would return the family to where they belonged.

The area in which the Janzens were living was the source of crude rock salt for refineries. Locks in the channel dug through the hills along the shoreline were opened periodically to allow the salt water to flood the land. The blistery heat of the summer sun evaporated the water, leaving a layer of hard dirty rock salt behind. Young Franz's job was to break up this layer, one to two inches deep, and push it into piles. Even unrefined salt would find a ready market once they left the area. Dad told young Franz to take his next pay in salt rather than money. He told the young girls to sew small burlap bags large enough to hold about ten pounds of salt, so they could help carry it.

When the local police pounded on the door and demanded that Dad come to the office to have his travel papers checked, everyone felt panic, but he came back in good spirits. They had found his papers, given to him by his Jewish friend, in good order.

Everyone moved into action, for they had a workable plan. He returned to the local government office and asked for travel permits for the entire family. The officials agreed to let Mrs. Janzen and the children leave but forbade the father to quit his job at the mill. This wrinkle didn't deter Dad. The mother and children would leave with Dad and the father would try to elude the authorities and come later.

The captain of a freighter hauling salt to Kherson agreed to take the family along in exchange for the cow. One morning at high tide, he came with a small boat to the shore where the family was gathered with their bags of salt, a few pieces of furniture, and personal effects. Mrs. Janzen and the children waded out to the boat. Dad and young Franz carried the dresser, sewing machine, and the salt high above the lapping waves. Then the sailors rowed the boat to the ship, where the family was helped up the rope ladder. They spread their few belongings on the deck and sat on them for the first short lap of the journey across the Black Sea.

At Kherson, the flourishing city at the head of the Dnieper River, the captain unloaded them and their belongings on the dock under a small wooden shelter. While the children ate their dark bread, Dad set in motion the second part of the plan.

"You and the girls stay here," he said to his mother-in-law, "while Franz and I go to the bazaar. We'll look for someone from Sagradowka to take us along. There'll be someone there, I'm sure." His words comforted the timid woman with the raspy voice. They were to guard the salt. It was valuable.

He and Franz walked up and down the narrow aisles of the market, bustling with people ready to buy or sell dried fish, cloth, carpets, baskets, pottery, and leather goods. They mingled with the buyers, looking for Mennonites in the familiar visor cap, open shirt, and wooden sandals, and listening for the familiar sounds of Low German. But they saw only Russians and Ukrainians and heard only Slavic dialects.

Then, near the cattle market, Dad glimpsed several ladder wagons, a type of carriage unique to the Mennonites.

These wagons had an extended undercarriage on both sides on which ladders were mounted at sloping angles to form a hayrack. At the end of the harvest season, those ladder wagons were converted to regular wagons again. The Makhno bandits had found their large capacity useful for looting during the revolution.

"Franz," Dad shouted, "that's what we're looking for— come on!" The wagon owners were standing nearby discussing the sale of some hay with some Russians. When Dad greeted the men in Low German, they knew at once he was one of them.

"I want to get a family to Friedensfeld, Village Number 3, in Sagradowka District," he explained. He offered them a small bag of salt in exchange for a ride for the family. The men agreed. They knew about the salt shortage in the interior and drove to the dock to load the Janzens, the sewing machine, the dresser, and the salt. Each wagon took several people.

After a long jolting ride, they arrived in Friedensfeld, where the villagers came to the roadside to watch the procession until it stopped at the relative's home. Over the next few days, many people came to welcome the family back, for they had known them earlier. To Dad's disappointment, however, few, including the wealthier people, brought food and clothing for the undernourished family. Perhaps too many refugees had already returned from great distances and food supplies were limited. Father Janzen arrived by himself several weeks later.

At last Dad's job was done. "Now you take over," he said to Mother's brother. He had found what was lost and restored it to its rightful place. He could hardly wait to take to the road again, but this time the direction was eastward and home to the wife waiting for him. A man from Rosental (Mother insisted his name was Penner) who had come to trade wheat for flour at Friedensfeld gave him a ride back home.

About a month after he had first left the house by the windmill, he too trudged up the lane to the Funk house, through the gate, only this time it was late. Mother was already in bed. He knocked at her window, and she rose quickly to let him in.

Mother asked one question, "Did you find my parents?" "Yes," he said, and dropped onto the bed, exhausted. In a few minutes, he was asleep. Mother began preparing a meal for him, as she would the rest of their lives whenever he came home tired and weary from life's constant struggle. Food was her way of showing comfort and love. He had given. Now she would give. She went down to the cellar to bring up some fresh stewed apples. She set out slabs of fresh bread, baked just that day. It was fortunate they had baked that day instead of waiting until the next. She let him sleep for a while. He ate when he woke up, then they talked.

"Where did you find them?"

"Prairie, more prairie, and still more prairie. Then fields and fields of tumbleweed. There, beyond the tumbleweeds, I found your family."

By that time the village of Rosental and surrounding communities sensed the coming winter would be grimmer than the ones they had survived thus far. The crop had been almost a total failure, and few people had been able to store food for an emergency. By November people no longer had enough to eat, and more and more beggars dragged themselves from door to door begging for a little *Khleb*. Some villagers gave generously, others withheld the food for themselves. All tightened their belts as they stared at empty cupboards, cellars, attics, and granaries and wondered who would be left in spring to tell the story of this winter.

Mother saw her parents the fall of the year that Dad found them and again in the spring of 1923, just before she and Dad, Frieda, and Annie (born that January), left for America. No one knew it was the last time they would see each other as parents and daughter and share a piece of bread.

And my father? He had learned another lesson in speaking the language of the poor and landless, which strengthened his desire to leave Russia. In spirit he moved ever closer to the oppressed and away from the rich and powerful. His ambivalent feelings toward these who were his brothers in the flesh—but also in the Spirit—was produced more by rage for their apparent insensitivity to the needs of the poor than by greed for himself. He had explored firsthand with the Janzen family the self-hatred and guilt of the poor who must depend on others for daily bread. He had experienced with them their fear of pain and suffering. He knew their shame at having to depend on others for sustenance.

He went to America looking for a place, a people, a community. He didn't know you have to have a place you can call your own before you can leave it; otherwise you are an alien and a fugitive. He had never felt that the Mennonites in Russia fully accepted him as he was, landless and lefthanded, so he left. Though the little Russia of Blaine Lake made him one of their own, he felt an obligation and a tie to the Mennonite world across the river who had lived his story and he theirs. He couldn't break that tie.

He felt most comfortable in the store, hands in his pockets, talking to his Russian friends, or preaching to them in their church. He deeded us, his children, the heritage of this compassion for the oppressed and the need for personal convictions, but also an ambivalence about who we were. Yet, who can say that isn't the experience of every immigrant child?

11
Waiting for Summer

THIS LITTLE pig went to market,
This little pig stayed home,
This little pig had roast beef,
This little pig had none,
And this little pig cried, Wee-wee-wee,
All the way home.

---

*B*EFORE I HOPPED onto the swing, I unhooked my garters. In a few seconds, my uncomfortable lisle stockings
had become neat brown doughnuts around my ankles.
I knew I'd have to pull my stockings up before I went into the
house, but why wait another day to feel the delightful freedom of bare legs after months of long underwear, heavy
stockings, and clumsy boots? It equaled that airy feeling
when I was allowed to go somewhere on well-trodden snow
paths in winter in only shoes. I pumped the swing back and
forth vigorously. Summer would soon be here.

Summer activities lined up in my mind like goslings behind their mother. We enjoyed many small pleasures that had
no price but were priceless. What greater delight than catching fireflies in jars? My sisters and I usually trudged to a small
nearby slough to collect tadpoles. I had saved several low tin
cans, like sardine tins, for making mud pies. The extra-fine,

dry dust of the Depression years made the best mud for mud-pies, smooth like rich cream, and dark like chocolate. My friend and I decorated our earthy concoctions with small stones, twigs, flowers, and fine sand, then we baked them in the sun.

Maybe Mona and I could make ourselves some new horsehair rings when the horse dealers brought in wild horses to be corralled in the next block. Dangling our feet from the top rail while watching the horses being broken made an afternoon gallop past. We loved lying on our backs on the prickly grass and telling ghost stories or watching the northern lights scamper across the northern sky. Maybe this year I would learn to ride a bike, even though the only bike I had access to had a huge metal basket in front and belonged to the store for delivery purposes. And it was a boy's bike at that. But I was ready.

On the first warm evening, the neighborhood kids would all be out for a long siege of "Run, my good sheep, run." Two daring team captains, well-matched as to leadership skills, provided more excitement than any modern TV spy thriller as they led their sheep to safety under the very nose of the enemy. When Mother called us in to wash up before going to bed, we tore ourselves away reluctantly.

There were many other wonderful things to look forward to in summer. First we cleaned the winter's accumulation of dirt from the playhouse, actually a little shed built onto the garage, and got Mother to wash the curtains hanging over the one small window. I hoped that year maybe my sisters would consider me old enough to manage the control panel (actually a thick board with heavy nails partly driven into it) when we pretended the playhouse was a magic flying machine. After we persuaded Mother to lock us into the playhouse and she provided us with sufficient food for a year's journey, we set off on journeys to exotic lands and far corners of the universe. The control person determined where we went, how close to danger we came, and what new adventures we had. Maybe that year Frieda and Annie wouldn't shoo me away from the control panel even if I couldn't come up with exploits as imaginative as theirs.

Yes, I was waiting for summer, for new activities, for new opportunities, even for the pleasure of sitting in the fresh air of an outside toilet instead of the smelly inside one. But I and many others waited for much more during those years of the Depression.

The rain to fill the slough never came. We children no longer squished the mud lazily through our toes after a summer shower. As we played in the dusty corner lot, the dry grass crackled beneath our feet. We picked few raspberries from the neighbor's overhanging branches. Our carrot patch came up thin and straggly. We gasped if we spotted a copper someone had lost in the cracks of the wooden sidewalk. We might spend several hours trying to fish it out, working with a variety of tools. A copper was a small fortune.

Mrs. Padovilnikoff, our neighbor, hoed for long meaningless hours in her unproductive garden. Just to keep her few spindly plants alive she hauled pail after pail of water on her little wagon from the village well, losing much of it on the bumpy journey.

Dad's worry lines deepened as many more bills were added to the spike on the kitchen cupboard. Our debts grew. Fewer of his customers paid with money; more and more handed over relief vouchers.

The farmers gathered outside the elevator to have their seed grain treated with copper sulphate, their hands rough and red from the harsh chemicals. Grasshoppers flourished despite the absence of growing crops to feed them and the presence of poisons to prevent the young from developing.

During the duststorms of 1931-1933 and 1935, Mother laid damp clothes along window ledges. She placed a mat over the door sill to keep the dust from filtering in. Not until many years later did I realize that covering a set table with a cloth was done out of necessity, to keep the dust out, not as a rule of etiquette.

Those were the years that flour and sugar sacks became the staple cloth of necessity. Tablecloths, tea towels, sheets, pillow cases, dresser scarves, petticoats, pajamas—all were made from well-bleached sacks, sometimes with the Robin Hood logo parading across our backsides.

Those were the years I longed for a ten-cent box of crayons instead of always having a five-cent one, but even that request made Father look troubled. I longed for slithery thin underwear that fell to the floor in silken puddles instead of having to wear the bulky bloomers and heavy petticoat that acted as a winding sheet when I walked. Mittens were made out of socks, which we, and other children with similar apparel, hid behind our backs or stuffed into our pockets. One year Mother insisted I wear her made-over black coat to school because there was no money for a new one, and I had outgrown my old one. I refused and wore a thin skating jacket all winter, even in thirty-below-zero weather.

One Sunday when I was about eight or nine, we drove miles and miles to Glenbush, where there was a church like our across-the-river church and where Tina, a former friend of Mother's in Russia, lived. We got up terribly early and drove and drove on the narrow dirt roads north through bush country. We ate breakfast on the way—sandwiches and such things with sweetened lemon tea.

We arrived on time at church. It was a large, white frame building with simple lines, built on the pattern of all early churches, with a graveyard adjoining. I could have taken bets, if our family had not thought of betting as sin, that we would be almost the first ones there, even though we came the longest distance.

Regardless of where you went to an across-the-river church, you knew where to go. Men and women had separate entrances, and there was always a little room for each gender to hang coats and hats. Everyone knew where to sit—men to the left of the preacher, women to the right, old men at the front of the men's side, little children in the front on the other, middle-aged next, and young people on their respective sides at the back. Preachers sat in a row up front with the song leader.

After church we went to Mother's friend's house, a big farm with good food. About the middle of the afternoon, we left to visit another friend of Mother's, whom she hadn't seen since the Russia days. We came upon a homestead site that even my inexperienced eyes could tell wasn't adding up to making a living. A stark one-story box built with rough unpainted boards squatted in the middle of the bare farm site. The screenless windows were covered with only wrinkled green shades. On the table was an oilcoth, worn through at the corners. The kitchen smelled sour. The whole place reeked of squalor and despair.

Mother told us to go outside and play. Our hostess's children were all too small or too different in temperament to join us. We were sophisticated village children, accustomed to energetic interaction with our neighbors. They were decidedly farm children, whom circumstances had pushed back relentlessly into becoming silent observers of strangers in their midst. I moved about gingerly, hating to stir up the dust that settled thickly on my Sunday shoes and socks. I walked around the barnyard, stepping carefully over fresh cowpies and chicken droppings. I peeked into the barn and found neither the smells nor the sights interesting.

Mother was in the house with her hostess, watching the preparations for the evening *Faspa* on this warm, dusty Sunday afternoon. She saw her friend had made a big bowl of gooseberry *Moos*. This was something she also made, but her friend's *Moos* had huge, ugly, gray globs of cottage cheese floating in it, and looked like a mammoth cooking failure.

She knew my strong dislike of gooseberry *Moos*. With clumps of cottage cheese added, she had no doubt the other children would probably turn up their noses at it also, especially if we had to eat it out of the unwashed dishes the adults had used, a common custom in the Old Colony in Russia. She was perplexed. Her children would shame her if we came in, and she was having a hard time relishing the idea of eating in the sour-smelling, fly-specked kitchen herself.

By then we children were sitting in the car, moping, waiting for something to happen. Mother came out and told us to eat the leftover egg sandwiches from breakfast. She didn't think we would like what was being served inside. She took with her the pan of chocolate cake she had baked in a halvah tin, our standard baking pan. She would tell them inside we weren't hungry. How she persuaded her hostess we weren't of the eating variety of children, I don't know. We didn't go back there for many years.

During those hard years, Dad came home with all kinds of stories. He told us of the young boy caught stealing school lunches. The school trustees set up a watch system to find the culprit. They whipped him severely and took him to his home, where he lived with his elderly grandmother. There they found the cupboard absolutely empty. Then even the men wept.

Sometimes when Dad and I walked home from the store, he told me to go ahead. He'd be there in a minute. Once I looked back to see him pull loaves of bread and ring bologna out of a sack and give them to one of the men spending the night in the livery barn with the horses. The man immediately tore the sausage and bread into chunks and handed it to the other men. No, I wasn't so hungry that I would ever stand and chew bread and bologna in the middle of the street on a cold night. The hungriest I could remember was the half hour before the bell rang for noon, when my stomach growled as I watched the clock.

The Depression was a time of desperation, especially for men who lost their life's savings in the 1929 stock market crash. Each year finding a livelihood became more difficult, until hope itself fled. Before I became a teenager, I could list at least eight or nine suicides in our small village.

One morning as we walked to school as usual, I noticed the blinds still down in the lumberyard we passed on the way. At noon we came home to find out the manager had shot himself during the night. Another time the father of a friend hanged himself from an upstairs window. Another chose the barn.

As the despair deepened, people, including some of our across-the-river relatives, opted for another province. They moved to British Columbia and Ontario. A country school teacher whose wife became sick after they had already packed their belongings to move brought her and the children to our place for rest and recuperation. Mother washed all their much-mended clothes. She gave the weary wife and mother tender, loving care. Dad looked worried as he told us that their car engine was tied to the chassis with a chain. The family had mountain driving ahead.

Yet each morning before we went to school, my little red-haired immigrant mother read us a Bible story and prayed, "Thank you, Lord, for food, clothing, and shelter. Give us this day our daily bread." We children sped through our table prayers to get at the food faster, but she prayed slowly, deliberately, as if she were talking to someone, as if she meant it.

During those long, dry summer days, I watched the freight trains rumble by our yard. At first only a few men lay on the roofs, then more. One day, as I trudged to the store, a group of them had found their way to the bench by the bank building. During the dirty '30s, the passing freight trains discharged scores of jobless hoboes into our small community. Old young men in worn clothing begged door to door for a meal. The bench at the bank corner was crowded with limp bodies barely holding up the empty faces, out of which peered tired eyes. Cautiously I eyed the vacant, waiting faces. They didn't belong in my world. I didn't want them to enter my world. Yet poverty in various forms became our guest, sometimes our intruder, sometimes our enemy during the next years.

One early summer afternoon, someone knocked at the screen door. "Mom, come, there's someone here!" I called as I stared into the face of a Depression hobo. Solemnly he handed Mother a note from my father in the store. "Give this man something to eat, then let him chop some wood." Dad believed he saved a man's pride if he could work for the donated food or money.

Mother invited the man in, showed him where to wash, and prepared some food. She set the table as carefully as she would have for us and served him standing, as was her Old Country custom when guests were present. What was she thinking? I don't know.

In the Ukraine before the Revolution, in some villages beggars had multiplied to such great numbers that the village elders decided to restrict begging to one day a week. Friday became *Prachadach* (beggar's day). Dressed in rags, with gunny sacks thrown over their shoulders, the beggars went from door to door, from early until late. Each was armed with a heavy stick to drive away dogs. Some people even made special beggars' food, plainer than usual. During and after the Revolution, the number of beggars increased.

Maybe Mother thought of the times her own mother cooked a thick mixture of flour, water, and salt during their hungry times, and of how the family of twelve children took chunks of the cooked dough and dipped it in the bowl of melted butter set in the middle of the table. Maybe she thought of when they first landed in Canada, homeless, penniless except for twenty-five cents which they spent for soap. They were warmly welcomed by friendly, gracious hosts.

Mother and Dad's first night in Canada was in the home of some Schellenbergs. In the simply furnished home, Mrs. Schellenberg, wearing a clean white apron, set the table for the evening meal, spreading it first with a smooth white tablecloth. Mother had watched and wondered whether the day would ever come when she would serve guests from a snowy-white tablecloth, wearing a lacy white apron.

The next morning their hosts showed Mother and Dad around the house, including the playhouse for their children in the brief tour. A playhouse for children—how unique! But the striking aspect of that playhouse was its white curtains. Would she ever have white curtains for her own house? Would her children ever have a playhouse? That dream kept her going.

Mother and Dad never looked back to Russia. They had chosen to live in Canada, where there was the possibility of fathers working instead of going to war, of mothers cooking with real food instead of grain husks, of children traveling to the moon in their imagination in playhouses with a curtained window instead of huddling in bedclothes all day because of the cold.

I watched from the doorway. Our beggar smelled rank. His clothes looked grimy and worn. Why had Dad picked him? After eating hungrily, he chopped some wood and left.

Something happened as I watched the homeless man eat at our table. Sharing our "daily bread" with him, the bread Mother prayed for, made life whole for a moment. The darkness of the Depression would not defeat us unless we let it.

That man was not the only stranger to sit at our table or sleep in our beds during the '30s. Our woodpile, on which my little brother liked to stand and shout, "My mother is a royal cook," grew that summer because of hobo help. One day two Polish immigrants, newly arrived, were sitting at the bank corner. When Dad went by at his usual fast pace, he noticed these strangers and asked where they were from. They asked for a job. "Dig my garden," he said. Mother made them a meal. Dad paid them some money. Years later they returned to tell him he had saved their lives. They hadn't yet eaten that day.

But I shall never forget that first hobo, sitting at the head of our table, silently eating our food, and Mother serving him as if he were an invited guest, not just a beggar with a gunny sack over his shoulder.

I understood Mother's words much better the next morning as she again prayed, "Thank you, Lord, for food, clothing, and shelter. Give us this day our daily bread." The Depression was still with us. I was still wearing flour-sack underwear. I didn't own a ten-cent box of crayons. But now I knew she wasn't just saying words.

Years ago, in northern Saskatchewan, when the frost covered the windowpanes with furry ridges, we children rubbed a spot clear with a forefinger until the bright, shining winter world again came into view. Each child could view the outside world through a private peephole.

My memory peephole recalls the little joys that highlighted those difficult years. The rare gift of five cents bought a big bag of jelly beans, a huge Sweet Marie bar, or a soft drink. Perhaps once or twice a summer, we each tasted an ice cream cone, licking the edges carefully to preserve each precious drop.

Then when winter arrived and snow blanketed the earth, the despair always changed to hope—at least in the hearts of the children—for Christmas was coming. An aura of peace and goodwill hovered over the struggling community for a little while and lifted it out of its despair, giving life a glory even the poor could enjoy. The village people moved closer to each other for spiritual warmth. Every Depression child knew Christmas was about love even if he or she didn't know the right words to talk about the incarnation of Christ. Christmas meant joy and hope. Without it, even if we had it only briefly, life would have been a perennial, arid emptiness.

The spot I have rubbed on memory's pane becomes suddenly very bright as I think of Christmas and the happy way it dominated our lives for several weeks. First came the Eaton's mail-order catalog with its storehouse of wonders, then the carol singing in school and church and the practicing for the annual programs. The agenda included the creation of gifts—out of more flour sacks as well as papier-mâché, tin cans, and oilcloth. We picked names in various gift exchanges and hoped rich girls or boys would get our names. We hated Dad's teasing regarding the gift St. Nicholas might bring even while we loved it. Mother baked several varieties of cookies—*Pfeffernüsse*, ammonia, oatmeal, and icebox—and stored them in the frigid veranda. Some years she baked fruitcake. If we managed to eat twelve kinds at twelve homes, it meant twelve months of good luck.

I took my turn filling the bags of Christmas treats for the children of the country schools that their school boards ordered from my Dad's store. "Katie, come help fill another order." One-half pound of nuts, one-quarter pound of mixed candy, one Japanese orange. All children knew that no matter how slim their parents' resources were, they would each get a bag of treats at school.

The Depression years grow brightest in my mind as I think of the many times we, as a family, listened to Dickens' *Christmas Carol* over the radio or of how we strung popcorn or painted walnut shells for tree decorations. The Christmas tree was decorated with real candles, which we lit once or twice a season under the careful supervision of our elders.

Intermixed are memories of the Christmas concerts in the United Church and our wholehearted attempts to create joy with poems, plays, songs, and the coming of a real Santa

Claus. Christmas was joy, not piety. Costuming was important at these concerts, even if the costumes were only borrowed bathrobes for the wise men and shepherds and cheesecloth and tarnished tinsel for the angels.

Occasionally we tasted a little ecumenicity by flocking to the Catholic Church to see if their program was any better than ours or if their candy bags were any bigger.

At last Christmas Day arrived. We were made of sterner stuff than those who reserved this gift-opening event for Christmas Eve so they could sleep late the next day. We waited until the real day. There was the early morning rush to find the gifts placed beside the breakfast plates we had set out the night before. We could see at a glance what the gift was, for nothing was ever wrapped in those early years. We reveled in these gifts of love—unmerited, sometimes bought at great sacrifice, given for no other reason than that it was the celebration of Christ's birth.

Then as swiftly as it had come, Christmas was over and we returned to our routine. Grownups worried about next year's crop and finding enough money to pay the bills. Children hoped maybe in the new year there would be enough money for a store-bought dress or a bicycle. Though the summer might again be dry and fruitless, the memory of Christmas joy eased the pressures and made life whole for a while. Each year after Christmas came spring and seedtime and hope. *Maybe this year. . . .*

12

The Hunger Years

OLD MOTHER Hubbard went to her cupboard
To get her poor dog a bone,
But when she got there, the cupboard was bare,
And so the poor dog had none.

WE CHILDREN PROBABLY weren't as hungry as the hoboes who came to our door for handouts during the '30s. Being hungry had two meanings for Mother. There was the good kind of hunger we children had before meals, when we would come in from play and shout the Low German rhyme, "I'm hungry, I'm hungry, my stomach is so empty it is being slung back and forth."

There was another kind of hunger, the kind she meant when she admonished us to finish our plates: "Some day you may not have enough." It was the kind of hunger she meant when each morning she thanked God for giving us food, clothing, and shelter. The kind of hunger Mother was talking about turned even very fat people who claimed their obesity was due to glandular problems into thin shadows of their former selves. Mother never forgot the hunger years in Russia.

Mother and Dad never talked as much about those famine years from 1921 to 1923 as they did about their experiences working at the mental hospital, living at the mill, or coping with war and revolution. These were the silent years of their lives, never revealed until much later. It was as if, even after they came to Saskatchewan, the hunger years remained a dull ache; the drought years in Canada were a constant reminder of that experience. Did they fear the desperate years in Saskatchewan would continue the pattern they had learned to know in the Ukraine—a pattern of hardship, hunger, lost loved ones, and sometimes death?

In the spring of 1921, after the anarchist Makhno bands quit their plundering, murdering, and terrorizing in southern Ukraine, collectivization of farms was just beginning. The last of the grain in some Mennonite colonies and the surrounding communities peopled by Russians, German Lutherans, and Catholics had been used. Little seed and few implements were available for spring planting. Everything of value was gone. The livestock the bandits had stolen was not yet replaced. Farmers who had previously proudly owned eight to ten well-groomed horses now hitched a couple of leftover nags to a couple of cows to plow and sow the little seed. Sometimes a husband and wife added their strength to that of the animals.

Bread prices and taxes rose astronomically. Czarist money was worthless, and the new ruble inflated more and more. During normal times, the poor found the taxes hard to pay; now it was impossible.

Mother and Dad and little Frieda were still living with Dad's mother near the windmill. The drought of that year was widespread. A little rain came at Easter and a little a few weeks later, then none until August. Wheat and other grain crops were stunted. Grasshoppers devoured the little plants struggling to maintain growth.

By the end of October 1921, the famine was in full force. Families realized they would harvest next to nothing. The stores were empty. Many immediately put themselves on rations, and those people survived better than others.

Dad listened to the men gather as usual on the wooden

bench next to the mill in the early evening. They stared dejectedly at the long, narrow farms usually heavily dotted with large strawstacks—signs of a good harvest and the family's wealth. Lively talk about farming practices was reduced to monosyllabic exchange.

Granaries, attics, and cellars, usually full of field and garden produce, stood empty that fall. Even fuel was in short supply because the meager crop produced few vine trimmings or little straw to burn in the large wall ovens. In good times the farmer distributed the winter's accumulation of manure over a small hard area, packed it down with threshing stones, dried it in the sun, then cut it into slabs for fuel. But without livestock to produce the manure, even this was no longer available.

The livestock were fed whatever was available, including in some extreme situations the straw from the thatched roofs. Finally the animals had to be slaughtered and eaten before they died of starvation.

When Dad's neighbors talked to one another as they looked at the watermelon and pumpkin vines and the gooseberry and blackberry bushes with their small, pinched fruit, one would say, "We have baked no bread for three weeks," and the other would reply, "And we for four weeks." Each day there was less and less good food in the Funk household to feed the eight people, which included three growing boys (my father's brothers), his one sister, his mother, and Mother, Dad, and Frieda. The rack suspended near the ceiling which usually held the big loaves of *Bulki* was empty.

People pursued supplements to stretch their remaining grain. Bread was baked with anything that might yield nourishment, like beets, leaves, corncobs, linseed or sunflower seed cakes, pumpkins, and barley. As the need grew even greater, sawdust, chaff, and Russian thistle seeds—tiny black seeds—were added. Dad sent the chaff at the mill through the milling process again to glean more flour.

Few people planned the usual hog butchering with its accompanying jolly social activities. People dropped the tradition of *Faspa*, eaten leisurely in the middle of the afternoon with lots of good-natured visiting.

The day's activities concerned themselves with attempts to find food to keep body and soul alive. Yeast was seldom available, so some turned to making sourdough, but it was difficult to keep sourdough going without white flour to add to the starter. They could not buy salt, and few had lye and fat to make into soap.

The family in the mill house sat down together to their simple meals and wondered if, in a few months, they would have to eat what some of the poorer people were resorting to. Mother and Dad heard of people boiling the hides of butchered animals for the nutrients in them. Some even shot crows.

A friend saw a villager driving his weakened horses down the street. One creature collapsed from hunger and died. Before the man could cut it loose from its traces, the beggars (there were many), pounced on the carcass, dismembered it, and carried it off. The man sat and cried, unable to do anything.

People who at one time appeared smartly dressed in fine woolens, pleats, tucks, and laces, showed up with patches on top of patches like all the others. Bandits had cleaned the community of all good shoes and boots, so as the cold weather approached, the villagers turned to all kinds of makeshift footwear to cover their feet, from the familiar sandals to old felt boots, rags, and galoshes. Growing children appeared most ragged, for as they outgrew their clothes no new ones could be purchased. Sometimes burlap bags were fashioned into trousers.

No dogs howled at night as formerly. Stray dogs and cats ran about at their own risk. Anyone who saw a dog being led by a rope around its neck knew the creature's end. Pets were carefully watched by those who still had a cat to kill mice. No roosters crowed to greet the morning. No horses clip-clopped smartly down the street. Once Mother saw the neighbors cooking something in a big pot in the backyard. She went over to investigate and found they had cooked several cats.

Even travel was affected. Men and women journeyed long distances by foot. If something had to be hauled, heavy wagons were replaced by small carts made of a few boards on an axle to lighten the load for the weak horses.

Some of the neighboring peasants turned their children out to beg, for they no longer had food to give them. In some Mennonite villages, instead of one day a week being beggar's day as was formerly the custom, every day became *Prachadach*. The villages became crowded with refugees, who stood at the door with toothpick limbs and swollen abdomens asking for a little bread. Housewives gave what they could. When householders were down to the last flour in the sack and could give only water or clear soup to beggars, they closed the door and then the windows, for the beggars peered in wherever they could to see if someone was eating.

At the beginning of the terrible times, church functions were scheduled less often. No one had energy to attend. Each Sunday morning the elder read the list of sick and dead. Usually death was caused by typhus, spread by lice, or hunger. The congregation sat silent, pale, unmoved by his announcements, as if all feeling had left them.

With the beggars came the thieves. With no police or working government, the people were unable to control this new plague. The village watchman, a regular, familiar sound and face, no longer made his rounds. A committee of villagers was organized to deal with the thievery and to punish as need be. Sermons constantly admonished the people to not steal and to share with others, but here and there a father or a mother could no longer hold out or trust that God would provide and resorted to stealing. The anger and power of the men in control sometimes overcame them also, for a few persons were beaten so severely they died.

As the fall turned into winter and the people could see no hope of help coming their way from anyone, some became bitter, closing their hearts and spirits to any words about God and his love. Typhus, the killer of the previous year, returned and killed off the most susceptible, usually the older adults. Orphaned children were distributed among several families, for few homes could add six or seven mouths, even small ones, to their table.

Poor families looked around them for saleable items they could exchange at the bazaar for flour or grain. Dressers, dishes, watches, clocks, any jewelry that was left, implements, even the last few animals were sold if the selling meant food for a few more days.

The Funk windmill was not functioning often those days. To stand on one of the thoroughfares meant watching funeral processions, beggars, hungry neighbors go about their business. One day the bodies of an older couple, wrapped in sheets, so they looked like mummies, were being transported on a small horse-drawn wagon to the graveyard. The day was windy and the sharp breeze whipped the graying beard and hair of the blackened faces of the old man and his wife. Her *Haube,* given to her on her wedding day, nearly blew off. Had life's storms not punished them enough in life? Why were they punished after they were dead?

Berry picking for food was almost futile. But each time Dad went, he hoped to find some dried berries someone had overlooked or to snare a gopher or kill some crows with a slingshot, so they would have little meat on the table. Gopher meat tasted like pigeon meat. More and more men and boys were spending time in the woods at this activity. How long had it been since Dad had eaten a full meal? He felt the weight of providing for the eight people around his table, but even as he added his prayers daily to those of the rest of the family, each day the meals became simpler and smaller. He had swept every corner of the mill for stray kernels. The mill had never been cleaner.

As Dad searched in the underbrush, he came upon a small child. She was three or four, a little older than Frieda, standing silently, eyes big and solemn in a face that looked world-weary. Her legs, scratched by the underbrush, were like spindles. Her feet and abdomen were puffed up like pillows, indicating that she was in the final stages of starvation. He wanted to give her something, but his pockets were empty.

"What is your name?"

Before the child could reply, her mother, thin and haggard, obviously a Russian peasant, grabbed the child and moved back into the bush. Dad had no courage to keep looking for berries. His Frieda would be in that situation before long if he didn't do something.

Only that morning, before he had left for the mill hoping against hope some customer would show up, Frieda had not toddled to him as she usually did when he left the house. Instead she sat slumped over on the blanket on the floor. When he had called to her, she had tried to get up but couldn't. He had seen Mother look at Frieda also. Her eyes had filled with tears as she turned away. Their child no longer smiled or laughed when he took her on his knee to give her a ride, or to recite the Low German rhyme in which he stirred porridge vigorously in the palm of her little hand: *"rea, rea Jretje, jev dem waut, jev dem waut . . ."* Both Dad and Mother knew what the trouble was.

Something else had to be sold. The Kruger clock with the green and gold face as large as a plate-sized *Blintz* and the long brass pendulum and heavy weights was long gone. So were other items they had brought along from Kronstal when they returned to Rosental after the Makhno bandits left.

What did he have of value? He rubbed the wedding ring Mother had given him at their formal engagement. Tomorrow he would sell it. He returned home.

When he entered the door, Mother handed him her wedding ring before he could say a word. Both knew rings were not needed to make a marriage that had survived the chaos of revolution, death, and disease. Neither of my parents ever wore a ring again, even after they could afford several.

For a while the local village authorities set up soup kitchens for the very destitute, but eventually they were discontinued when large supplies of food were no longer available. At the Christmas program in church, each child was given a small cookie or a walnut, nothing more. The year closed on a hard note, yet for many their early hardness softened and people started coming to church services, asking for spiritual help. In the midst of physical starvation, spiritual food abounded and hundreds were converted. Each evening at the services more people gathered to listen to sermons on the need to live as Christians, to care for one another, and to trust, even though it seemed that God had turned his back on them.

In the midst of the famine, the rumors increased that the American Mennonites, their brothers and sisters in the faith, were planning to send help. Negotiations were in progress. For some, there was always the fear that help would come too late.

Early in 1922, about February, the Mennonites had assurance that help was on its way. The forerunner of Mennonite Central Committee, the American Mennonite Relief Administration Committee (AMRAC), had been organized. Carloads of flour, rice, cornmeal, and other foodstuffs, as well as clothing and implements, were on their way. Food kitchens would be set up in most villages to prepare one hot meal per day for the most needy. One such kitchen would be opened in Rosental/Chortitza, where Mother and Dad lived. Those in charge were looking for volunteers to help work in these kitchens.

Mother looked at little Frieda. Workers would be given double rations, not as pay, but to give them strength to work. She knew she could cook for large groups because of her five years of experience at the mental hospital. Dad had managed the field hospital kitchen warehouse in the army.

Dad's mother went to the local officials to tell them her son and his wife were prepared to help with the work in the kitchen. Dad couldn't come himself because he was busy in the mill and Mother was at home with Frieda.

Mother waited impatiently for her mother-in-law's return, spinning silk on the spinning wheel to kill time. She had started her own silkworm colony in the empty attic. Each day she and Dad's brothers brought the growing worms mulberry leaves, then finally large branches. Their chewing sounded like soft rain falling on the trees when she walked into the attic. She baked the cocoons in the oven to kill the larva, then unwound them in boiling water. After it was spun, the silk made good thread, otherwise unavailable.

Finally her mother-in-law returned. She had asked for the jobs for them.

"Did you tell them I had experience cooking at Bethania?" she asked.

"No. We started talking about the rations and who they would be for—and it slipped my mind."

Disappointed, Mother returned to her spinning but prayed she would be able to accept God's will, whatever it might be. This had seemed such a great opportunity. The work meant food, especially for little Frieda, whose thin face stared at her from her cradle.

The next day two official-looking men strode up the hill to the house by the mill to see the young couple who wanted to cook.

"Can you cook?"

Mother explained her credentials without trying to seem overzealous. She knew she was a good cook, but she hadn't been able to prove her skills for some time. She and Dad were hired on the spot. The next day they moved their few personal belongings to the relief kitchen.

On March 13, 1922, the food arrived and was unloaded in the warehouse. People stood and gawked at the many sacks of flour, rice, and beans such as they had not seen for months. The kitchen and dining room were housed in the former public school, which had been closed for some time.

The old skills, learned at Bethania, came back in a hurry. Serving eight hundred to one thousand people each day was a challenge. Besides Mother and Dad, there were two men to carry water and three girls to help with the cooking. That first noon when the doors swung open to admit ration-card holders (children, elderly people, sick people, pregnant women), Mother watched as the people, in their ragged clothes and patched footwear, sat down to eat. After the prayer of thanksgiving, the little children bit into the wonderfully soft buns, something some had never tasted. Mother prided herself that at the Rosental/Chortitza kitchen the rice was never burned in the big kettles as she heard it was at other kitchens. The children scraped bowls clean, then licked them.

In a matter of weeks, the watery eyes and hollow cheeks changed. The frail bodies of the children began to put on weight. Even Frieda regained her former frisky spirits and was toddling around, getting underfoot as Mother and Dad worked preparing the meals each day.

In the spring of 1922, the prospects of a crop looked better. The donated seed was planted. Mother planted some potatoes that had rotted on the passage to the Ukraine and found they grew well. When she wanted to dig them up, she left empty-handed. Someone had been there ahead of her.

The food kitchens continued throughout the summer. Government became stronger. There were fewer reports of robberies and murders on outlying farms or on roads, although these still were common. Mother and Dad heard of a whole family who were cruelly whipped, and then suffocated with the reins of their horses. A man and his companion on their way to Kherson had been murdered.

Those who received money from America bought horses and livestock. AMARC supplied tractors and other implements. The spring of 1923 looked even better. On January 17 my sister Annie was born with a local midwife in attendance, but Mother and Dad kept working at the kitchen. As they worked the talk about immigrating to America grew louder and louder. They were determined to be part of that group. They wanted to go to a place where there would be no more hunger, where they would have a chance to choose the condition of their lives. But in Saskatchewan, the land of promise, some of the old conditions returned. Hunger and need had followed hard on their heels to Canada.

13

Becoming a Woman

LITTLE Jack Horner sat in a corner
Eating his Christmas pie.
He stuck in his thumb and pulled out a plum,
And said, "What a good boy am I!"

MAYBE KATIE could go . . ." Dad continued pushing the last drop of soup toward his mouth with the large spoon he insisted on using. He was in a hurry to get back to the store so his clerk could go to lunch also, only we called it dinner.

"What's it about?" Mother stopped at the stove where she was getting some more soup from the big pot.

"Cooking, cooking—learning to cook. Let one of the girls go . . . costs nothing. Agriculture department is doing it . . . two weeks. Begins August 3, I think—I'll check."

He finished his soup before Mother could refill his bowl, then shoved it to the middle of the table with both hands, a gesture indicating he was finished.

"I don't want anymore—got no time." She wanted him to take time to eat, but he walked out the kitchen door the short half block to the store to deal with the afternoon trade. He had said everything there was to say.

I said nothing as I finished my bowl of soup with a normal-sized spoon, then, bread pudding with a still smaller spoon the way real Canadians did it. Mother said nothing, but I knew she was thinking. The other children said nothing. Such matters were not settled by discussion with parents. They told you what must be done, then you did it.

That's the way it turned out.

The summer before I began eighth grade, Mother and Dad decided their third daughter would attend a government-sponsored cooking class. I was the daughter too young to work at anything useful, like dusting furniture for rich neighbors had they existed. I was too old to play with paper dolls, which already overfilled the shoe boxes in which I housed them. So I was elected to learn to cook. But there were other reasons I was chosen, related to me and yet not.

First, it was high time I grew up and became a woman, which in essence meant learning to cook. But not English-style cooking, which had no sense of what tasted good. My father, who came from a tradition of good eating, not necessarily good nutrition, couldn't stomach his mashed potatoes without nearly drowning them with ladles of thick brown meat gravy. Mother became ill if she heard of a hostess serving naked boiled potatoes to guests with only a little juice from the roast to pour over the meat.

"Can you imagine? Boiled potatoes and no gravy." Her heart wept for the diners. Her tone evoked forlorn potatoes, the magnificent fruit of the vine, and her favorite vegetable—all lying cold and uncovered on an equally cold plate.

Dad believed all good wives should know to bake bread, darn socks, and milk cows. Some day I would be a wife. It was time I learned another skill on the road to womanhood.

By some fluke of circumstances, I had made it to this stage of life without ever having baked a cake, a pan of cookies, or a batch of bread. Mother was an expert baker and depended on ingredients such as regular weekly deliveries of two-quart jars of farm cream and homemade butter to aid her developing reputation in the community.

Growing up during the Depression didn't mean growing up without food, only without money to buy prepared foods, fresh fruits and vegetables, and ready-made clothing from the store. My cooking skills at the time were meager. I could set the table and carry to the strawberry-decorated oilcloth (which we children had helped select) whatever Mother and my two older sisters had already cooked. I could go to the garden with an empty grape basket and fill it with peas, beans, carrots, and radishes; wash them outside with water from the rain barrel; and prepare them for supper. I could slice bread, hacking away at the huge wheat boulders even though my slices looked immoral compared to Mother's even slices. That made Dad ask testily, "Who cut this bread so miserably?" as he tried to butter the lacy end, only to watch it crumble before his eyes. I could, if need be, boil eggs and potatoes. I could even fry the potatoes over a wood fire, which had its own vagaries, without burning the bottom layer.

But I didn't know how to mix ingredients—a spoonful of this and a handful of that—for a savory dish that drew raves from the family.

My lack of cooking skills might be explained by arguing I had never had a chance to learn to cook. I had two older sisters at home who preferred cooking to cleaning and a mother who was the reigning monarch of the kitchen range. But that summer I too was to have my chance to become a fully-developed woman. I knew how to darn socks. Milking cows was not within the range of possibility, for we lived in town. I was to be initiated into the sacred rite of cooking. I was to attend cooking school.

There was another reason I was chosen to go to cooking class that year, one a little more remote from baking bread. Someone in the family had to go. It was as simple as that. Showing up at cooking class was a little like the way we attended the local church on winter Sunday evenings when we couldn't attend our own across the frozen river. Someone had to represent the Funk family to show our support.

As he sat warming his wool-sock-clad feet in the open oven, Dad excused himself from attendance by complaining about the hard week he had had at the store. Mother couldn't understand English, at least not the ecclesiastical English used in Sunday evening sermons to mollify life-weary listeners. The older girls had homework to finish; the younger two children had to go to bed. Katie, the middle button, could go to church and represent the family. Katie could also go to cooking school.

She could show by her presence that the Funks were graciously appreciative of the new land which had pressed us warmly to its bosom and given us the opportunity to make a new life. By sitting in one of the half-empty pews and listening to the preacher extol his text in the semi-darkness (lights were always turned down for the sermon as in a theater, although I couldn't understand why), I showed we Funks were supportive of good causes.

Good causes or great causes, especially those arranged by the government, needed our full-hearted and full-throated support. Cooking school was a great cause. Katie could go; she was the only one of the three oldest sisters who didn't know how to cook.

Early in August, one Monday morning, when the sun was already greeting the day at a decent hour, I pulled my favorite print dress with blue flowers on a tannish background over my head, tied the tie-back belt, folded a clean, starched bibbed apron (frilly tea aprons weren't acceptable), and skipped down the wooden sidewalk to the cooking school being conducted in the United Church sanctuary. The whole building consisted only of the sanctuary and a tiny entrance.

Crowded into the front section of the church, the place where the pews and raised platform and choir section parted company, were a dozen other undeveloped young females. Clad like me in temporarily crisp cotton dresses, rolled hose or socks, and heavy leather oxfords, sent for reasons only their parents knew, they lolled about, waiting for the action.

Our instructor, a serious, dark-haired woman, heavy in body, thin in voice, oozing confidence and sweat, called us together to the front benches to explain what we would be doing for "two exciting weeks of cooking."

For supplies, the farm girls brought produce like milk, butter, and eggs. Our teacher supplied us with recipe books and encouragement, both of which we needed. We cooked over the sickly, orange-tipped, blue flame of a kerosene stove that reeked.

The idea was that what I learned at cooking school in the morning, I would duplicate that evening for supper. Dad probably expected lessons in plain cooking, like soup, bread, and oatmeal. Our teacher, a resident of the Big City, probably intended to expand the cooking repertoire of us poor, underprivileged immigrant children from our standard fare to more exotic dishes. Unfortunately, she didn't know that most of our mothers could plan and produce what their families thought were prize-winning meals faster than she could open a cookbook—and without a recipe or a rack of measuring cups and spoons. Mother made the best rolls in town and knew it. Her chocolate pudding tasted like ambrosia out of heaven's cafeteria when she brought it in from nestling in a snowdrift half the morning.

Monday evening's blancmange was my first culinary offering to the family. I made it for dessert for supper—a whole pot full. We always had lots of milk.

"*Woat es doaut?*"

"Blancmange." I tried to get the family to use the right French accent, to snort it through the nose.

"It tastes like nothing!" I dropped blancmange from the potential menu for future meals.

Other milk desserts followed—Delmonico pudding and jam trifle. A little better. The family admitted that floating custard had a slight charm—very slight. That delicacy was followed by rhubarb chutney. Rhubarb grew more profusely in our yard than dandelions. Without words the family decided they could do without chutney. The jar remained full. Next came baking powder biscuits and golden sauce.

The *pièce de résistance* was custard sauce. "Probably the most widely used milk custard is the palatable custard. Combining the two nourishing foods—milk and eggs—in an appealing way, custards are particularly suitable to serve to children and convalescents," stated the cookbook.

I learned there are cooked and baked custards. Both curdle if overcooked. "To ensure smoother texture, care must be taken in cooking custard as overcooking will cause the mixture to curdle." I put a big X beside those lines. "Four eggs are necessary if custard is being made in one large baking dish. To test custard, insert a silver knife in the center, and if it comes out clear, custard is cooked."

At our class in the church sanctuary, we made baked custard, an unknown entity to my European family, who preferred desserts to be more substantial than slippery, sweetened eggs solidified. We poured custard sauce on waffles or brown Betty pudding. Alone, custard had no character. At cooking class, I watched over this gourmet delicacy like a cat over new kittens. As it baked, I poked it often with a silver knife until it looked like a gored pig, but finally the knife came out clean and I pronounced the custard done. We students and teachers ate it and agreed it was edible. I planned to repeat the prize performance at home.

But I should have remembered that information about custards and convalescents. My family was not a bunch of invalids languishing in bed but a group of hungry people who had spent the day carrying hundred-pound sacks of flour, playing ball, and washing floors.

About five o'clock I offered to make baked custard for supper. Four eggs, three cups of milk, some sugar, and a little nutmeg. I watched it carefully, cocooned by its own pan of water in the oven. My inserted knife came out clean—no curdling! Success! I was learning. I was becoming a woman. I served the custard to the family. The applause was not deafening. They preferred Mother's homemade lemon pie with mile-high meringue.

My tapioca pudding got slightly better ratings.

The Saturday after I graduated from cooking school, in the midst of the usual rush to get enough cooking and baking done for Sunday, I declared I wanted to do some Sunday cooking because I knew how to cook. I had had enough of dusting ledges, chairs, and stairs. I had a cooking certificate. I could handle adult female responsibilities.

Mother eyed me carefully. Against her better judgment, she said, "Make some mayonnaise." That was something only she made. She was willing to test my cooking degree.

We needed a double recipe for potato salad and similar foods she'd be preparing during the next week. She felt pressured to do all the tricky cooking herself to save time, money, and her reputation. Under her expert hand, the dishes always came out perfect. I was asking for a piece of the action.

I was confident I could cook mayonnaise as well as I could play hopscotch. I measured liquids and solids, broke eggs, and stirred. The old enamel double boiler was perilously full of the pale yellow liquid with specks of mustard floating on top. I panicked when I realized it would take more than a week's apprenticeship to get that huge ocean of eggs and milk to coat a silver spoon. It required divine help.

Sister Frieda was baking a Lord Baltimore cake. When someone was baking a cake, the rest of us walked softly and the cook carried a big stick, because sudden movement caused the cake to flop. Flopped cake with its heavy rubbery base was transformed into pudding or some more solidly nourishing everyday dessert.

But for visitors, we needed a light fluffy cake that fell

apart at the touch of a knife, with mountains of seven-minute frosting artistically swirling on the top and sides so guests fell to their knees in admiration. Sometimes Frieda or Annie baked two or three cakes before one turned out right, but sacrifice in the interests of perfection was expected when flour lacked quality control. Mother and the girls would examine the flopped cake, smugly and solidly settled on the bottom of the pan. Then Mother would say determinedly, "We'll have to bake another one."

I stood at the old range and stirred and watched the fire. Frieda wanted a medium fire for her Lord Baltimore cake. I needed a fairly hot one to keep the water in the double boiler bubbling briskly. I called for more heat. I pleaded for more heat. Frieda, in her graciousness as older sister, yielded. Annie rushed outside to the woodpile for some kindling and pushed it into the firebox. The flame roared into action. Suddenly, without warning, the yellowish mixture whirling in the pot separated before me like the Red Sea into watery liquid and heavy, ugly curds. But I had not prayed for it to divide. My stomach and brain separated also.

"It's curdling!" I SOSed to anyone nearby with compassion for a new cook.

Mother flung me aside, grabbed the pot, whisked it off the stove, inserted the egg beater, and turned that handle like a demon until the mixture regained some semblance of flocked velvet.

I sat in the corner on the stairs and wept into my apron. I was a failure as a cook and as a woman. That week each time the mayonnaise appeared on the table with its granules of overcooked egg I recalled my disaster and took huge helpings, gagging on every mouthful, but ready to get rid of the evidence of my failure as swiftly as possible.

I renounced cooking for life. I was not yet a woman. The next Saturday I went back to my usual weekly task of wiping dust from ledges, stairs, furniture, and under doilies.

14

Sin with a Small "s"

RING-A-RING o' roses,
A pocket full of posies,
A-tishoo! A-tishoo!
We all fall down.

---

*B*Y THE TIME I was about thirteen or fourteen, the stories about Russia stopped or I quit listening to them. They belonged to the past, to a time I wanted to forget. I was becoming a Canadian. Too much of life lay ahead to spend energy on what had happened years before. We had been shut up too long in our little immigrant world. It was time to move beyond Main Street to new experiences. The whole family jerked ahead into the new life, sometimes carrying, sometimes dragging, sometimes being borne by our immigrant heritage.

Mother and Dad became Canadian citizens five years after they arrived in Canada. With reasonable use of the language, they were less reluctant to exchange the old ways for the new, which meant Canadian clothes, haircuts, activities, and customs. My sisters and I were ready for the challenge.

I longed for a pair of shorts. The fad for beach pajamas and whoopee pants swept by me and my sisters before we totally grasped that clothes had styles. But shorts—now that was a different matter. We girls wore Mother down with our begging until she allowed each of us to sew a pair of shorts. I didn't tell her that I wanted them because movie stars wore them.

Dad looked at his three oldest daughters with some consternation when he came home for lunch and saw this generous and daring display of thighs.

About two o'clock, Jakie rushed home with the message: "Get those girls out of their pants! *Prediger* Kroeker is in town." Across-the-river customs, where ultimate judgment lay, had won out again. We three girls were all discreetly attired in modest cotton print dresses when the preacher came to the house for a cup of tea.

Dad was usually not overly concerned with what we wore. However, when he was in the buying mood, he did like to buy for Mother and us girls what he thought were attractive garments. Mother usually made our clothes big—we would grow into them. Several inches of extra cloth on pajama bottoms flapped around our ankles for years before another sibling inherited them and found them also too long.

Once Dad had bought Annie, who was short, a yellow ochre dress that was unusually long. Mother refused to let her shorten it. Maybe Mother thought it had to be long when it was my turn to wear it, for I was taller though younger. Annie objected but wore it to a school concert where she tucked her skirt in at the front, thinking no one would notice that the back dragged like a bridal train. Mother saw what she had done and sent up word for Annie to untuck her skirt. Annie complied under duress, convinced that everyone thought she was wearing her nightgown.

The girls across the river all had long hair and wore stockings instead of "worldly" socks. When we arrived at church with short hair and socks, Mother had some explaining to do. Frieda was the first to get her hair cut and have a machine permanent. She had to work in the store late on Saturday evenings and had no time to fix her hair in deep finger waves like the girls across the river. Mother defended Frieda to the crinkle before the minister who planned to report her to the church board.

One day the unmarried woman across the alley told Mother about a wonderful new invention—the home permanent. Olla wanted to earn a living for herself, not be dependent on her parents, so Annie was offered as the lamb to have her hair curled by this wonderful new product. She went across the alley early in the afternoon and stayed late, while we waited for a curly haired beauty to return. About six o'clock she came into the kitchen, sheepishly, her hair still as straight as a ruler.

There were several categories of sin in Blaine Lake. SIN, all capitals, was never discussed in front of children, particularly innocent children like us who lived protected lives. Adults whispered about such SINS when they were alone in their bedroom, or after the children had gone to sleep, or when they thought the little pitchers had closed their ears. But what adults didn't know was that little pitchers always had open ears when it came to hearing about the woman who lived above the cafe and offered services of some kind to men; about the man who ran away with the hired girl, "and now she is pregnant"; or the preacher who visited too late and too long with a single woman; or the schoolteacher who had to go away because she was pregnant.

Another kind of Sin with a capital *S* could be talked about a little more freely, like the fight between John S. and his wife. She came into the store on Monday morning with a black eye, a big bruise on her forehead, scolding and crying. John had come home drunk, and because she couldn't move fast enough to suit him, he had pushed her against the door. Boozing and wife beating or desertion of wife and children for the wild blue yonder were discussed openly.

We heard about the underling who embezzled his bosses' funds and about the day laborer who had been paid his year's salary and gambled the money away in one night in the beer parlor—a phrase always said with a negative slur. We were never allowed—nor, horrors, did we want to go—inside those dens of iniquity. Sometimes we surreptitiously watched men sitting outside on the hotel veranda playing cards, perhaps even gambling. Some of the town women had bridge clubs and played whist in the afternoon, but we knew that was Sin with a capital *S.*

All of these things might happen in Canada, but we knew enough not to get close to them—or to white slavery, whatever that meant—against which the preacher across the river sometimes hollered. But we heard about other sins, those with a small *s.* We of human bondage and frailty who lived in the midst of those sins might yield. We heard about lipstick, red nail polish, swearing, smoking, drinking, dancing, and attending movies. Begging for treats at Halloween wasn't sin. It just wasn't done in our family.

Then there were the little taboos like socks, which we always wore (and how wonderful it felt in spring to remove the heavy cotton, wool, or lisle stockings and feel the fresh breezes whip around our bare legs), shorts and halters, and especially slacks. A little modernization was all right, but nails dripping blood pointed directly to sin, so I compromised with colorless nail polish and powder, which Dad wasn't sophisticated enough to spot.

But I never expected to get hauled back to Old Country customs in another area. I needed a new Sunday dress, so I picked out a delicate shade of peach rayon chiffon and a pattern with a cowl neckline. Mother shook her head but agreed to work with the slithery, thin material. I think she enjoyed the challenge of sewing with these new materials. Such cloth had never been available in the Ukraine. Of course, such a style and color as I had chosen was unthinkable in a culture where women wore only dark, drab colors. She added a slip of similar color in heavier material.

I had visions of myself floating down the stairs. Better still I imagined I would drift regally into the across-the-river church, and every young man would gasp with inner pain at this image of loveliness in flowing layers of peach chiffon entering his awareness.

When I waltzed proudly down the stairs on Sunday morning in my peach chiffon creation, Dad took one look and the roof beams shuddered. No daughter of his was going to church naked. I thought I was ravishingly beautiful. He thought I was lewd. He roared. I cried. Mother arbitrated, but in the end I wore my old cotton print. Later Mother sewed a complete liner for the offensive garment, which I hated wearing from then on.

But Mother herself was beginning to discover that she could open doors to the new world. She dared to use the mail-order catalog, the book we loved almost better than any other, for it gave us a glimpse into another world and brought that world closer to ours.

Sending off the winter order to Eaton's or Simpson's was always a big event. First came the long discussion about what was needed, then the repeated paging through the catalog again and again to find the best buy. We read the descriptions of articles to ourselves and to Mother. Was it available in the right size? No. Then another look. Shoes were always a problem. If after two tries the shoes still didn't fit right, we traced the outlines of our feet and sent that to the mail-order house.

After many hours spent studying the catalog, Mother courageously ordered a hat. "Get one with a big brim," said Dad. "I like big brims." She was wearing a big-brimmed hat when he first met her. But she wanted one of the more stylish ones without a brim. Size was also a problem, for she wore a bun. What was she to do about the bun with some of the close-fitting hats? Off went the order for a brown felt hat with orange feather decorations.

The day the big box arrived, we had to wait for her to open the package and pull the hat carefully from its nest of tissue paper. She tried it on. "Does it look good?" We knew better than to express strong opinions at this stage of the procedure.

"I'll try it on again when Dad gets home."

Another try-on session. Dad was noncommittal. Mother was uncertain. "It doesn't look good." Sadness tinged her words. She knew how Dad hated customers who brought back merchandise. Yet she had too much money tied up in that hat—and now it didn't look good. The picture in the catalog and the reality didn't match. Her mouth formed lines of determination yet sorrow. She examined the hat carefully again from every angle to confirm her decision. Yes, it had to go back.

Any item returned included a long letter of apology written by my older sisters, for Mother believed real people worked for these companies. They weren't faceless entities. The fact that the cloche didn't look good on a person with her kind of forehead wasn't their fault. She had misjudged the picture. She offered her sincere apologies with emphasis on the words, "I didn't wear it."

Ordering from the catalog, of course, meant that you might meet the same hat coming toward you next Sunday on several other women. These mail order companies, among the most accommodating businesses, were happy to serve the thousands of customers who, though they didn't know English well, were learning the art of buying by mail.

Another stage in Mother's coming out was buying a Spirella corselette from an agent who came to the community occasionally. I don't know how Mother heard about her, but every few years she walked to the local hotel to be laced into a prototype that pushed and pressured rebellious flesh to a new resting place. Then the agent measured her for her own garment.

Mother's reasoning? She needed the extra support such a garment gave her after having had five babies. Our reasoning? Short, plumpish, conscious of her weight, she liked to look smooth and trim in her Sunday clothes. The $15 she spent on a corselette didn't begin to match what Dad spent on all kinds of gadgets that fascinated his curiosity.

She never shook her staunch belief in the authority of teachers, a carryover from the Ukraine. The teachers were always right. If they said we had misbehaved, we had misbehaved and were promised a spanking at home equal to the one we had gotten at school. Teachers enjoyed wisdom not entrusted to ordinary people. Mother did not feel capable, at least in the early years, of conversing well with them so Annie was told to have the grade one teacher tell Susie to drink more milk and to quit sucking her food from the roof of her mouth.

In time, however, as a new Canadian, Mother believed it was her duty to become acquainted with her children's teachers. This meant inviting the teachers for tea after school as other mothers did. Sometimes the guests included the wives of village VIPs, like the local banker, senator, and lawyer. For this major event, the house was cleaned more thoroughly than the usual Saturday cleaning. The menu for this high tea was reworked several times. Once, at the last moment, she withdrew watermelon because she feared the teachers might consider it an insult. Russians, or any immigrants, were usually given lower social status in our community. The teachers she had invited were all British, so the watermelon the Russians loved was taken off the list.

Invitations were sent to school via us children: "Mother would like you to come to tea on Thursday after school." Next came the actual food preparation—puff pastry, cookies, rolls, little sandwiches, to be served with heavily starched napkins and an embroidered teacloth on the tea tray. Food was Mother's way of expressing herself. Every guest in the home was offered at least a cup of tea. Her rolls were spoken for at food sales before one of us carried them to the bake sale. We liked to report back the comments of those present, which she accepted, not with pride, but with satisfaction. We girls helped serve tea in the parlor to the honored guests and hurried to the kitchen to clean up the crumbs and nibble at the cake. I might cut a small triangular sliver from one edge. The next sister felt obligated to straighten the line. It was remarkable how much cake could be eaten when no one ever ate a whole piece.

Living alongside us in this pressure chamber to make it as Canadians were all the other immigrants, stumbling, going down to defeat, rising again, drifting, looking victory briefly in the face, then falling again. Even as a child I sensed that the community enjoyed a rare sense of camaraderie despite the distinct social classes. The English (meaning anyone who was from the British Isles) and the High Russians headed the pack. We, according to my thinking, were next. Then the Slavic people, of which there were many kinds. Then the poor whites, metis, and Native Americans (whom we knew only as Indians) in descending order. What gave a person prestige? Education, money, position, and good character. That was where Mother and Dad came in. They and many others were respected for their honesty and trustworthiness.

The immigrant population had risked leaving behind a country, relatives, sometimes fully equipped households, to make a new life in Canada. They had brought with them only a few small artifacts, a language they couldn't use freely and were tempted to discard for English, and values and attitudes toward life which they tried to fit in somewhere in our little village. A number had risked homesteading, not to get rich quickly but to find a modest living impossible in the country left behind. They knew nothing was deserved. All was grace.

It was a time of experimentation on many fronts. One local Russian woman decided to begin an organization called

Canadian Girls at Work (CGAW), in which we girls would make crafts. Our uniform was a sand blouse with a red and white polka dotted kerchief and dark skirt. We fashioned crepe paper cushions, silk thread flowers, embroidered squares, stuffed oilcloth dolls, and doorstops made out of catalogs, while an older girl read to us from *Elsie Dinsmore*. One year, as our masterpiece in Depression art, we raffled a large replica of *The Age of Innocence* in a heavy papier mâché frame gilded with gold and silver paint. The ugliness of the frame haunts me to this day. We held a bazaar to raise money for the poor. I don't think the organization survived much beyond one or two years.

The across-the-river-church was left in the dust during the winter as our social activities swung into high gear. School socials on Friday nights couldn't be excelled for enjoyment in our teenage years. After games of all kinds, we feasted on baked beans, pie, brown bread, and dill pickles. Sometimes we gathered to play with great intensity that exciting new money game, Monopoly, in the home of someone fortunate enough to own one. Tensions ran high for a few hours, unaccustomed as we were to handling money. We Funk girls had to leave at a decent hour for our beds, yet I found myself unable to sleep after having brushed shoulders for several hours with temporary tycoons and beggars.

It was always a problem to know how much of this new culture to accept and how much to reject. The church across the river determined some of the boundaries for those of us living in Blaine Lake. But where the categories were unclear or without precedent, we knew we could establish a case with Mother and engage in the activity without guilt. We never went to movies in the Palace Theatre, but we could go to school movies, shown after school on Fridays for five cents. These were travelogs and early films like *Les Miserables* and similar classics. The teacher selected these movies, and the teacher was always right. So we handed over our hot five-cent pieces and slipped into the full classroom to sit two to a seat to watch black and white films jerk across the screen. The projector frequently broke down.

We attended the chautaquas set up in a large tent on the ballpark to watch the films there, often cowboy-and-Indian films and "educational" lectures. We rushed to the Palace Theatre to watch Little Theatre and minstrel and amateur shows. The guiding principle seemed to be that we could attend any place that didn't have soft seats without committing small *s* sin. But one year I did.

The teacher was taking a choir to the city to sing in the music festival, an all-day affair. The choir would sing, eat in a restaurant—a real one—then in the afternoon attend the matinee performance of Nelson Eddy and Jeanette MacDonald at the Starlight Theatre. But we had to get permission from our parents. That was a Mount Everest undertaking.

Mother didn't know what to say. We reasoned. It was a good show, no dirty parts. Everyone else was going. The teacher would be with us. Finally, banking on the word of the teacher, we received Mother's permission.

We sang at the music festival and went flat, terribly flat, in the big auditorium. We heard the judge with an English accent pronounce another chorus as "bettah" but not because it was from the town of "Biggah." Our teacher probably felt worse than we did. Then off to a restaurant—all thirty of us innocents.

Next came the movie. I crept in with fear in my heart. This was a real theater with wonderfully soft seats and a ceiling that sparkled with stars. Would the world end? Was I saved? Was I committing a sin, and if so what kind? Big *S*? Little *s*? Had I been wrong to beg Mother so hard to let us go?

But the fragile beauty of Jeanette MacDonald and the handsomeness of Nelson Eddy made me forget my fears. I watched spellbound as they sang, riding into the sunset. I liked this kind of sin.

Another aspect of our Canadianization was attending the annual Dominion Day celebration. Each July 1 we didn't even have to ask to go to the annual Sports Day, held annually since 1915. It was a town holiday with games for children, softball for women and hardball for men, and ice cream and pop for anyone with at least a nickel to spend. We children were free to come and go without being questioned like we usually were, even if we only crossed the street to visit a friend. Even Mother came sometimes for a little while to walk around the grounds. It was Dominion Day, the day we celebrated being Canadians.

Mother's attitude toward her adopted country was always positive. For decades she and Dad voted for the Liberal Party "because Mackenzie King brought us to Canada," yet she insisted we all go to hear the Conservative Party prime minister R. B. Bennett when he came to our small village where one of his staunch supporters lived. At political rallies we high school students were always there to heckle or applaud the candidates. Mother was proud and grateful to be a Canadian. On Christmas mornings the whole family listened respectfully to the king of England when he spoke from London. On Armistice Day we either attended the service at the memorial or observed two minutes of silence at home. We owed thanks in all forms. We were living in a land of peace. We were Canadians—and proud of it.

15
Ah, Sweet Mystery of Life!

MARY, MARY, quite contrary,
How does your garden grow?
With silver bells and cockle shells
And pretty maids all in a row.

GROWNUPS HAD SECRETS, and they weren't telling. Not yet. So I enrolled myself in my own secret course in the Great Mystery of Life and pursued my studies avidly as time and opportunity allowed. The girls in my class at school worked hard at the course also, individually and together. We were like a junior CIA. Yet we were at all times equally ignorant of what we were trying to uncover. We spent recesses distributing bits of information gleaned from weekend eavesdropping, none of which provided conclusive facts about anything.

My own body wasn't much to look at just yet. Smooth and hairless like a plucked chicken, with two slight protrusions on the upper half of my torso and the generous hips of a Greek goddess, I longed for the slim figure of a movie star. I didn't want the abundant proportions of either an Aphrodite or a Leda.

When no one was looking, I stood in front of the mirror in the upstairs room shared by us four sisters and sucked in my gut. I hoped to recognize the potential for an hour-glass figure in the bottom-heavy potato sack facing me. I sketched hundreds of beautiful ladies with long, flowing curls, wasp waists, and sweetheart necklines on dresses bulging with luscious fullness, but imagination didn't help me. I didn't have enough on top to balance out the abundance at the bottom, and my huge appetite kept my middle well rounded.

The Great Mystery was made all the more mysterious because nudity was never practiced in our home. I had never even heard that it was possible to be completely naked. We always wore at least some clothes. I would have been as surprised to see a dog strolling in the backyard without fur as to see my father without a shirt or my mother in her underwear. No family member ever saw another member in any stages of undress, even in a small squeezed-together house without a bathroom. I learned to take a spit bath over the kitchen sink, almost in public, without offending anyone. I could undress and dress, using my skirt as a protective tent, shifting it from shoulders to waist in stages, as I performed my ablutions in broad daylight with someone in the room. I don't think it would have mattered if the king of England himself were present.

My desire for at least an idea of what the human male form looked like unclothed was frustrated at every turn. I had no more way of finding out what lay beneath those layers of bulky clothing than of baking a cake for Sunday dinner. Each picture of a classic nude in *The Book of Knowledge* had a figleaf discreetly covering what I most wanted to see. I knew that my brother stood up to pee because we girls sometimes sat down on what he missed in his hurried aim. This caused near-fratricide if the slippery pages of the mail-order catalog didn't do a complete job of wiping up. In winter, male bodies were encased in long fleece-lined underwear, extra pants, and jackets. Feet, smooth and reddened from their prison of heavy socks and boots, were occasionally put on public display when the owner looked for slippers.

In summer I sometimes almost got my chance at a riverside baptism, if I looked particularly hard at the male candidates clambering out of the river, up the bank, to the waiting towel or blanket held by a parent or relative. The moment of being immersed in the waters of death and rising to the glory of a new resurrection was lost to me as I examined these young men staggering out of the water, yanking at dripping, clinging clothes to hide what I was looking for.

We girls called the strange, pendulous things women grew on their chests (they looked like overfilled water balloons or even cantaloupes) "lungs." We found it easier to talk about them that way. "Bust" sounded far too grownup, "breast" too personal, "bosom" too literary, and "chest" too casual. So lungs they became. Men had extra little bumps on their chests just like women did, but women had a lot more. This extra needed a word we could comfortably use in our vocabulary even though we didn't have any words available because this was a part of the body never talked about in public.

My awareness that something happened to girls as they grew up that had to do with dripping blood fastened itself slowly in my consciousness. It carried itself along with no loud cheering, no generous smiles like there were for the first angel food cake that didn't subside in its pan like an unhappy soufflé. It was a matter to be whispered about behind closed doors. Mother may have wanted to tell us girls what lay ahead for us as women but lacked English terminology to discuss it, and we didn't know her German.

I knew my sister Frieda sometimes wore a peachy-pink rope-like belt. I could see this thing when her pajamas gaped, but I knew I wasn't supposed to be seeing it or to ask her about it. That was her secret, and I wished I knew when it would be mine.

The year I was in grade six, we girls talked about little else than "this blood" for a whole three months. When was "it" going to happen to us? What was it? It had tremendous pressure—one tiny drop of this special blood could force its way through ten to twenty thicknesses of cloth. Why it needed such penetrating power, I never discovered. But I knew it was super-powerful stuff, too hot to handle or talk about casually. If the boys wanted to send us girls into the cloakroom screaming and giggling, they only needed to holler "Kotex" loudly across the classroom.

Normally we had kindly feelings toward any teacher who took sick (grade school teachers were always women), for then we could visit her at her boarding place and see what she looked like off duty. Most teachers roomed at the local red-brick hotel at the corner near the railroad and ate their meals in its public dining room. That seemed a glamorous existence to those of us who had never sat on a counter stool in a cafe to order a soft drink.

One day when Miss McGregor was ill, three of us girls trooped across town to her room to bring her a get-well present. We were always collecting nickels for presents for sick teachers. Our parents must have been disgusted with us but didn't know how to stop the monthly events without letting us in on the Mystery. That late winter afternoon, in the semi-darkness of the twilight hour in our northern area, I saw a grimy, stringy belt, bunched up in a shameful heap at the foot of her bed, as if thrown there.

"Did you see that sanitary belt?" Meta asked me as we tiptoed out after leaving our present with our suffering teacher. I nodded. The Mystery was deepening. A woman's lot was connected with sickness.

In my secret school, I exhausted much energy figuring out how boys were manufactured. What happened between their legs where we girls had only pale smoothness? How did they manage their pants with something dangling between their legs? Didn't it bother them or get squashed when they walked? On which side did they tuck this cluster, whatever it was? How large was it? How small? Bathing trunks, even then, never adequately hid the presence of this dangling mass.

One day a friend of Mother's visited our home with her toddler, still in diapers. I sat outside on the blanket on the grass with Mother and her guest, enjoying the warm air and keeping a weather ear open for bits of information to enrich my life and contribute to solving the Great Mystery. Suddenly, without warning, I saw IT. I held my head very straight as if I were looking at the stars while my eyes steered carefully to where the diaper did not fit snugly. Some soft, gloppy, crinkly things dangled outside the cloth and a little thing that looked like a tiny, plucked chicken's neck dangled outside the cloth. The Great Mystery advanced a full step that day.

I knew the solution was drawing close as my bones lengthened and the flesh covering them shaped itself in new ways. The few novels I managed to locate that had more than simple romance in them talked about something wonderful happening after the lovers melted into each other's arms in the twilight. In one novel, the heroine said to her lover as they clung to each other in the deep grass, "I won't be afraid if you'll be gentle." I memorized the line so that when I found true love and marriage, I'd know what to say even though I didn't know what took place after the words were said.

Mothers and fathers slept together, but I saw nothing unusual about that. All parents slept together. It never occurred to me that one day two people who had once been total strangers and didn't recognize each other's underwear on the clothesline or their birthmarks under that underwear had to crawl under Aunt Martha's present of a patchwork quilt and find a compatible way of doing it forever after.

So I looked for pieces to add the finishing touches to my puzzle, not knowing whom to ask. Mother was too embarrassed and Dad out of the question. Dads were not interested in such things. Religious books, though titled *What Every*

Young Christian Girl Should Know, explained nothing. They talked in euphemisms about avoiding fornication before marriage and adultery after. I didn't know what fornication was to avoid it—it sounded too much like good-tasting poison. The dictionary offered little help in defining it other than as the "act of fornicating." I knew flirting and kissing and holding hands were sins of the rankest order, way up ahead of lying and stealing. Was it because a kiss created a baby? If a kiss could get things going, what about a deep look? I had to find out.

One afternoon as I tripped into the kitchen to dump my books on the table, one of Mother's friends was about to leave after their afternoon tea. As she walked to the door, her parting jab was "And now she has to go away." She saw me and clammed up, heading for the gate.

I knew I had made a killing that day. "Why does she have to go away?" I asked Mother the moment the door shut. I didn't even know whom they had been discussing. "She was flirting with the boys too much, and now she is going to have a baby." The conversation was finished as she turned to clear away the tea things. I didn't know how to continue.

Flirting was linked to making babies. Laughing with the boys, sidling up to them at recess, batting eyelids in their presence—it all led to only one terrible end.

One Sunday afternoon, as our family visited friends on the farm, I stumbled into the barn looking for the children who had been playing nearby. Dad and Mr. Franz were standing at the far end of the barn, near the closed door, where only a few stray rays of sunshine dared enter, examining a mare that had just foaled. The spindly colt stood nuzzling its mother, entire body trembling. But the mother horse—my eyes riveted on its rear end. It was one huge open wound, red and ugly, as if someone had hacked its buttocks open with a meat cleaver. The crevice extended for yards and yards.

Mr. Franz looked at me briefly, then explained to Dad that the mare had had a difficult birth, so the colt had been pulled out with a block and tackle. The equipment still hung above the horse. I looked and looked at the monstrous cut that drew me like a powerful magnet, then rushed out into the fresh air. Birth! Babies came this way—big holes torn in their mothers! I stood beside the barn door, not feeling the warm sunshine or hearing the meadowlark shrilling on the fence post or the children playing beyond the haystack. My stomach churned like it sometimes did in the car when I had to sit in the backseat and the road was bumpy.

What if I had started a baby? I had looked hard at some boys. I had smiled at them, even held hands just a little—kind of a sideways brush. Would I get torn up like this?

I picked my way to the car parked under the row of poplar trees in the driveway. Sitting on the running board, I repented of my sins. I repented ever having skated with the boys so much and encouraging Ricky to walk me home. I repented of fooling around with a couple of boys for a whole recess after Peter had grabbed my comb. I was obviously headed for deep trouble if I continued such behavior.

There, in the shade of the old Buick, I decided to accept anything as punishment—even wearing long underwear one more year. We girls hated long underwear. We knew all the other girls wore them in the below-zero weather, but we each had our personal campaign set up to persuade ourselves, the other girls, and particularly the boys, that we didn't wear long underwear.

Every winter morning I wrapped the underwear cuff tightly around my ankles before I pulled up my lisle stockings as smoothly as possible to make my legs look as if the underwear weren't there. But by noon the knees were already baggy and my underwear and stockings had drifted apart into shallow crevices and puffy layers.

There by the car I told myself I would leave my stockings

baggy so the boys would think me ugly. I wouldn't even complain about wearing four-buckle galoshes, which made my feet hot and heavy as I tromped the classroom aisles feeling like a prize Clydesdale. Whenever possible I left my heavyweights behind, envious of the few rich girls who wore fur-trimmed velvet overshoes. I promised myself that as long as there was danger of falling into sin, I would wear galoshes and cotton petticoats that clung to my thighs.

I didn't want to be sent away to some distant land to have a baby. Being sent away from the family seemed worse than having the baby and being ripped apart from stem to stern. But babies were such cute, soft things that I relented for a passing moment. Then I remembered the gaping hole in the horse and swore off my pursuit of the Great Mystery.

That spring Mother raised the issue of buying a piano. Dad's answer was "No!" He couldn't stand the *Geklimper*. Pianos tinkled. They lacked the robust character of a pump organ, mandolin, or even balalaika, which could tear the heart from its ribcage when someone played Russian folksongs in a minor key. A piano? No soul.

Then, as so often happened, Dad bought something without asking anyone for advice. He bought a piano. One day a group of strong men groaned this big brute of a player piano into the living room. It stood almost five feet high and about as wide with generous gingerbread trimming. A big box of rolls came with the instrument. We children inserted a roll, swung out the little doors at the bottom, pulled out the pedals. Then, until our legs tired, the keys magically fell and rose all over the keyboard to give us "General Sherman's March to the Sea," "Rustles of Spring," and many more.

But player piano music wasn't good enough. I wanted to make my own music to clean out the passions mouldering inside, so I picked away at the piano keys after school. But without lessons, I was doomed to emoting only little whimpers and sighs.

Mother promised to edge in a good word for me with Dad. By evening the deal was made. The $1.50 I earned working in Dad's store each Saturday would be added to another $1.50 Dad would provide to make up enough for music lessons. I had a toehold into the world of music. The Chopin in me was going to be given opportunity to blossom.

That next week I sang as I strolled down the sidewalk for my first lesson. I was in. Someday I would move my hands rapidly up and down the keyboard in time with the player piano and listen to an enraptured audience clap for my renditions of "Country Gardens" or "Rachmaninoff's Prelude in C Sharp Major." That first year of scales and little pieces made the Great Cause seem so much more wonderful. Every agony and ecstasy of first love were poured out at the piano. Constant infatuation was a necessity rather than a willful attempt to break a rule. Yet being in love had little or nothing to do with the Great Cause.

Misgivings about sexual identity drifted in and out as I passed through one of the puberty rites of every young person in our community—learning to skate. Mother sewed us skating outfits—navy blue jackets and pants of heavy woolen material. Dad paid for season tickets to the rink, feeling secure nothing could happen to his daughters when we were bundled up to the neck, skating in twenty-degrees-below-zero weather. We girls knew that though skating wasn't much good for finding out about shapes of bodies, it was good for figuring out feelings even if the thermometer slid downward.

"Why are you always talking to the boys at the skating rink? Why not talk to the girls?" asked Dad.

Yes, why not? Because you didn't go to the rink for exercise or to talk to the girls, but to talk to the boys and give them a chance to look at you. You could talk to the girls at school. You could exercise washing the floor or bringing in wood. We needed the boy's eyes on us as much as we liked to look at them to guess how they were wired and plumbed.

The rites of passage for every young boy or girl of skating age began in the waiting room of the rink at the edge of town. On the skate-worn benches and around the barrel oven we put on our skates, rested, warmed up—and waited. A girl scored if a boy asked to put on her skates or at least to tighten the leather thongs. She scored again if a boy asked to skate with her and scored even higher if a boy asked to carry her skates home.

No sensation equalled gliding out onto the ice under the canopy of glittering stars, a brilliant full moon, and crisp, clear air as the loudspeaker blared "The Skater's Waltz" or "The Beautiful Blue Danube" and a strong, male arm pressed mine close to him. Making my own music meant I could reproduce time after time these moments of romantic ecstasy on the keyboard; that made the many driven but short and vacuous infatuations bearable.

My music teacher, believing her pupils should show off their skills in public once they had memorized "The Happy Farmer," signed me up for the local amateur hour, patterned after the famous Major Boews Amateur Hour on radio. The concert, held in the Palace Theatre at the end of Main Street provided entertainment for local citizens during the long winter. Tickets were minimally priced—twenty-five cents. Entrants were attracted by the small cash prizes or gifts donated by merchants. Winners were usually popular citizens willing to make fools of themselves, or those who appealed to local sentiment by singing comic songs or cowboy ballads, yodeling, or performing a lively Russian dance with a lot of heel stomping and shouting.

We went to the amateur hour as a family. Mother and Dad sat discreetly at the back of the hall to show evidence of their reservations of the event. We children with our friends sat nearer the front on benches, leaning against a single slat which cut into our backs. We wanted a closer view of both friends and enemies performing. It was innocent fun, even

Dad agreed, to watch the stand-up comic go through his homemade routine and get no laughs except for not being funny.

The evening before my debut into the cultural world, I determined to make myself ravishingly beautiful. Shimmering waves cascading down my shoulders were beyond me. Such beauty exceeded my family's genes and means. I looked at my straight blonde hair and knew I would have to turn to our own hair remedies once again.

I cooked a new batch of waving lotion. I boiled one-half cup of linseed with two cups of water, then strained it. I glopped the thick mucous solution generously on my hair while it was twisted into knobby pincurls. Hair encased in that solution had the consistency of week-old cement but did permit a little spiraling, like that of a metal corkscrew. Once Frieda waved Annie's hair with that mixture and formed a finger wave as big as an ocean trough. Annie complained. She could cradle her whole hand in the wave. Beauty demanded the smaller waves of a gently rippling brook.

Saturday was always hair day, but I broke tradition that weekend and washed, then rinsed my mousy strands on Friday evening with the juice of a lemon (there were always lots of dried-up lemons in the kitchen cupboard) to make my hair squeaky clean and radiantly golden. Instead of pincurls, I set it in rags so I would have fat luscious ringlets resting on my shoulders. At thirteen, I preferred ringlets to straight hair, and it was easier to sleep on rags than on metal curlers. Once before, in desperation to have curly hair, I had gone around with my hair in rags for two days and two nights, almost like Jonah in the belly of the whale. But the result was no different than if it had been one night. So this time I began the curling process only one night early.

The next evening, to ensure beauty at least briefly, I took out the rags five minutes before we went to the amateur hour. I wore my new navy woolen dress with the pleated skirt and shiny glass buttons down the front. A tatted lace collar matched the elegance of my ringlets. I felt beautiful.

When the announcer called for "In a Country Garden," I was all demureness and innocence. I reveled in the hand-clapping at the end of my performance. It was a little sparse and came only from one section, but it was applause.

Back in the wings, as I was about to return to my seat, the emcee beamed at me, complimenting me on my beautiful playing. His fish eyes ogled me from my curls, now loosened to a thin wiener look, to below the tatted collar. His hand resting on my shoulder became an arm surrounding my waist and feeling me in places I had never been felt before.

"How about coming to the hotel for a little party?"

Me? Attend a grown-up party in the hotel where the teachers and salesmen stayed?

He whispered a sweet nothing in my ear like I'd heard in radio dramas. My curiosity wanted to say yes. I'd have lots to tell my friends if I went to a party at the hotel with a man—not just a boy in heavy winter clothes. My father's conditioning turned him down, but the emcee's invitation meant one thing—I was growing up. The bulges were forming in the right places.

Each Christmas vacation we girls went to as many parties as possible. Each family with teenagers usually sponsored a party at which we played games like Spin the Plate, Monopoly, and Forfeits, ate cake and sandwiches, and talked. One year the Forman family down the street invited Annie and me to a party, a genuine, almost-grown-up evening party.

We played our games. Then at about midnight, Dale and Hank cleared a little furniture in the living room, placed a record on the gramophone, and started dancing with some of the girls. Dancing was *verboten* in our family, and I hardly knew what to do. I was aware of Mother's strict rules against anything that led to perdition. But if that night could bring me closer to an answer to the Great Mystery, I was willing to stumble around with awkward boys to the tune of "Mexicali Rose" for a little while, and to endure their heavy breathing while we clutched each other's sticky hands.

When one of the older boys walked me the two blocks home at about two in the morning in the sharp, cold air, I felt like a princess riding in a horse-driven carriage even though I was wearing winter galoshes. I knew the way home, but somehow that wasn't the point.

I opened the kitchen door gently, hoping to head for bed in record time. Annie had just walked in before me.

There sat Mother on the couch. Dad was upstairs sleeping.

"Where have you been?" She was upset, not mad-upset, but hurt-upset. We had disappointed her. I knew it was useless to explain that the party had just ended. She said she'd never let us to go to another party if we didn't know when to come home. Annie and I crawled into bed, each with our own thoughts. As I lay there quietly under the heavy comforter, waiting to get warm, I relived the evening, the being held close, the journey home, the words. We hadn't told Mother we had been dancing.

Mother was the caretaker of our spiritual, intellectual, and cultural welfare. Dad looked after providing money for food, shelter, clothing, pianos, and guitars. He also worried whether there'd be a place in life for his four girls and one son. Would we girls make it, not having grown up the traditional way on a farm where we'd have learned to milk, bake bread, and stook sheaves? Mother worried about the spirit with which we would move down Main Street and out the highway leading to the city. Dad worried whether we'd be able to move out at all. That night my spirit was at the party, dancing down Main Street, ready to find out what lay beyond the corner, past the slough and the slaughterhouse beside it, and toward the city.

That fall when I began school, most of the girls had already started their monthlies and looked like females. We no longer talked about that. Lizzie's "lungs" were so big we joked she'd give herself a black eye if she didn't watch out. I was still waiting.

One evening I went to bed feeling crampy sick. Something tugged at my insides like a cat wanting out of a bag. All night I twisted, digging deeper into the mattress to bury this strange, dull ache, which wasn't enough to awaken Mother and yet too much to handle alone. Always we children waited until morning to disturb Mother if we felt sick, but Mother usually knew long before morning, having heard the creaking bedsprings. That night no one came to my bed to ask, "What's wrong?"

I woke feeling headachy. An unusual sticky dampness between my legs bothered me. I looked. Blotches of bright red blood stained my pajamas. I stared unbelievingly. I knew what it was but couldn't assent to it. I waited until the other girls had dressed, then went downstairs, hoping to catch Mother alone somewhere. I wondered why, if now I had become a woman, I felt so alone.

She came back upstairs with me after I had whispered my need. In her and Dad's bedroom, she showed me how to pin on a belt, where to find the homemade napkins, how to place soiled ones under the mattress so no one would see them. Next week she would remove the cotton batting lining and wash the outside cloths. Next week my batch of rags danced in the breeze on the line alongside my sisters'.

Mother had already bought me a bandeau and a girdle, which seemed more fitting to being grown-up than anything I had encountered so far. When we were children, we girls wore vests with attached garters. Now I had a real girdle, a grownup woman's girdle with stays to curb the roundness of my backside. Girdles caused trials too, but that was the price of beauty. One of the plumper girls in class had a corset that squeaked when she walked down the aisle. Most of the others had the type of girdle that rode up over time. Those girdles had to be jerked down periodically by grabbing through one's dress and slip a handhold of the heavy material at the bottom edge of the garment to reseat it. But I didn't mind that either. I knew that would soon become a reflex action, like men easing their pantlegs before they crossed their legs. They pulled up; I pulled down.

I was grown-up.

About that time one of the girls at school told me that babies were started when a man and woman went to bed. She had seen their dogs doing it. Her idea was like squeezing a piece of limp spaghetti through a keyhole, so I dismissed it.

Now I shared the mystery of monthlies with all women, one which we had to keep from the boys, but which they somehow were aware of. Someday I would know their side of the Great Mystery which they were keeping from us.

16
A Real Live Death

I STREW the twigs upon the ground,
The frozen earth I sweep;
I blow the children round and round
and wake the flowers from sleep.

DEATH CAME IN bunches that year, like grapes on a
vine. What seemed like years ago, there had been the
death of our grandmother, but it had never seemed
like a death, for it was only on paper. A letter from Russia,
edged in black, to Mother and Dad, stated what had happened, how it had happened, what she had said to her children before she died—about getting the milking done and
where the rope was to tie the cow. It was a death for Mother,
for it was her mother, but it wasn't really a death for the rest
of us, for it took nothing from our lives, even as our grandmother's life had added nothing to them. We had never
known her.

Then there was the death of the father of Dorothy, my
friend in school in fifth grade. That wasn't really a death either, for one day her older sister found him hanging by a
rope in the old barn by the slough. He was dead with his
tongue sticking out. Dorothy's sister had run screaming from
the place for someone to help her cut him down, and she
was only about seventeen. The next day everyone was talking

about it in school before the bell rang and during recess, but Dorothy wasn't there so she didn't hear us. Then after awhile she came back to school and life went on as before, only she didn't have a father.

One day I attended a real funeral, with a coffin, a body, a few flowers, a sermon, and mourners, real ones. The local United Church minister had died. He was an old man who always wore a gray wool worsted suit—to match his gray beard and hair, I thought. Maybe even his insides were gray. He looked so old to me. He walked all stooped over, as if his backbone had gotten tired. Yet he spoke to me with a kind, gentle voice, as if he were stroking a cat. My parents liked him and his preaching. Now he was dead.

I walked around the gray coffin lined with shiny, shirred material. It was set on chairs at the front of the church. I looked in. An old man who didn't look like the man I had known lay in the box, his eyes closed, his wrinkled hands clasped over his chest as if in silent prayer, like he sometimes held them when he prayed in church. Although the adults around me looked sad and teary, I felt nothing. I looked for the wart on the side of his face that moved when he talked. It was still there. This death and the dying of Mother's mother as it had been explained in that long, black-edged letter didn't match. Which was real death? What was dying? What happened before it happened? After? I didn't know.

One spring day Dad told us over our macaroni and sausage that a woman and her husband from the country church had been driving to town. Stories always got told like this, from the beginning. The fabric cover of the buggy had torn loose and its wild flapping had terrified the horse. The animal had jerked forward, pitching the woman over backward onto the dirt road. Her neck had been broken. The funeral would be on Sunday.

Dad took Annie and me with him to the funeral at the Russian church, about seven miles out in the country. Frieda,

Mother, and the others stayed home. Annie and I were used to sitting quietly through long services we didn't understand. We had attended plenty of services that were either all German or all Russian, but the service that day did not resemble the usual high-spirited Russian gatherings.

The strong female voices in the choir that usually carried the entire congregation along in jubilant hymns sang softly, mournfully, without even trying. I watched openly as a woman nearby wept in loud gasps, rubbing her eyes vigorously with a handkerchief borrowed from her husband's pocket. A man in a dark Sunday suit and white shirt, face darkened by the sun to the clear line where he wore his cap, sat with two small, solemn boys, each scrubbed shiny clean. They sat near the front, all rigid like the statue in the Memorial Park.

No one whispered across the aisle as they usually did. The preacher's voice sounded grim, though I could only understand the odd word.

At the graveside—a crude, oblong hole gouged deeply out of the virgin prairie—the coffin was opened for the last time. It was the custom. The woman who had wept in the church and some others cried in louder, even more violent gasps, clutching each other. The man in the dark Sunday suit stood dumbly, staring into space across the grave. Someone had taken the children away. Other men, unaccustomed to wearing stiff suitcoats, wore black crepe armbands. They stood near the mounds of dirt by the hole. They held ropes and were ready to do the men's work at the funeral. In the background, a few children played by the cars and buggies, their high shrieks piercing the adults' self-imposed silence.

Annie and I edged close to Dad, who stood near the dark, cavernous hole. Curiosity overcame me. I wanted to see a dead person—*that* dead person. I bent over the hole, over the coffin, with its missing lid, for a good look—and nearly tumbled in. Below me, in the semi-darkness that shrouded the body, I saw my mother lying quietly, eyes closed. Same oval face. Same auburn-red hair, parted and pulled back. Same pale complexion. Same well-defined lips.

Mother! My mother?

My heart thudded and twisted as if it wanted to leap out of its prison. My stomach churned. I felt my body shudder under the assault of this recognition.

Why hadn't Dad told us we were going to Mother's funeral? Was this the way it was done? We had seen her alive about an hour ago at home, sitting in the rocking chair by the dining room window reading the *Zionsbote*. She hadn't been feeling well, as I remembered.

Dad didn't look particularly sad as he peered into the hole with me, although he looked solemn. But then I had never seen him crying for any reason. Fathers didn't cry. Only mothers and children cried. I wanted to shout, to scream, to force someone to explain to me what was happening before the men lowered the lid and nailed it shut. Mother—my mother! I needed my mother. I wasn't big like my mother who could get along in this country without her mother. I hadn't outgrown her—not yet.

No one listened to my pounding heart, and I had no courage to cry out. The men in the dark suits and crepe armbands lowered the lid, then one man jumped nimbly into the grave and nailed the coffin shut. The others helped him clamber back out. I heard the dull thumps of shovelfuls of soil hitting the lid, soil that probably had never been disturbed before except for the original natives riding or walking over it. The mourners and sightseers, restrained yet relieved, turned and left. Annie and I followed Dad to the car, parked on the far side of the church.

Dad guided the car over the rutty dirt roads back to town, all three of us sitting in the narrow front seat. I sat rigid, cold, clutching my insides to keep from crying. Dad drove into the driveway of our yard as he usually did. Annie and I crawled out before he put the car away in the garage. He closed the garage doors and locked them, then he turned to close the yard gate.

There were patterns to our family life—doors were locked and gates were closed at all times. Some gates and doors were used a lot and some only a little. Our front door with its small strip of stained glass symbolized a life that might someday come to our family in this new country. We used that door very seldom, though it led to the parlor where the couch, the piano, the Victrola, and the large fern reigned in joint splendor. In winter the door was covered with heavy corrugated cardboard to keep out icy drafts, and couldn't be opened at all. The back door handled the family and even guest traffic. It led to Mother, the kitchen, and warmth. But we had been away, and now it was time to close the gate and open the kitchen door. I hesitated to enter.

I swung the door quickly. There stood Mother as usual, in her blue-checked dress and white apron. She was bending over the kitchen stove, cooking something for supper in the blue enamel pot.

"*Wie ging es?*" she asked, glancing up from the pot she was stirring. It smelled like cocoa. We often had cocoa on Sunday evenings.

I looked at her, wanting to run to her, grab her, hold her. But I stayed in the small entryway where we kept the wood, the snow barrels, the washing machine, and outdoor clothes. I took off my coat with deliberate movements, looking sideways at Mother. Mother was not dead, not in that box they had buried in the ground. That woman had been someone else's mother. I still had my own. But someday she would die. Someday I might die, and they would lay me in a box and cover me with dirt. Death terrified me, but not as much as the fear of being buried alive. What if they buried me in a coffin before I was so dead I would never come alive again?

Lying beside my sister in the darkness of the night, I

heard the clock strike ten, then eleven—and the story of the two young men in one of the German villages in the Ukraine who had died of typhus came back in many forms. In Russia when a person died, family members laid the body out on boards in the outside *Sommastoav*, washed it, then swabbed it with alcohol to preserve it until the relatives from neighboring villages showed up for the funeral. On the day of the young men's funeral, the men who came to take the bodies to the church noticed beads of perspiration on the forehead of one body. They listened for a heartbeat but found none. They placed a feather under his nostrils, but it stayed motionless. They argued back and forth about what to do. What if he were alive and they buried him? They tried to rouse him, but it was useless. Finally they buried him with the other one, convinced he was more dead than alive.

The thought made me burrow deep into the hollow spot in the mattress on our white iron bed. I imagined the young man waking in the darkness of his narrow resting place and hearing the dirt being thrown onto the lid. Plunk! Plunk! Another clod! Buried alive! His weak shouts had nowhere to go in the small dark space. I could feel his heart racing as fast as my own as the realization hit him. I nearly smothered in the tunnel I burrowed for myself in the covers that smelled thickly of sleep and human bodies.

Then, strangely, I forgot about death.

For many years, each morning before we ate, Mother read us stories from a German Bible storybook. I liked the Old Testament stories better than the New Testament ones. I didn't like the ones about Jesus being betrayed by Peter and Judas, then whipped by some other men and crucified on the cross. I tried hard not to listen when Mother got to that section, which was usually before Easter. As she read, I thought my own thoughts about the play we were practicing in school or whom I would ask to play Jacks or Knife with me at recess.

When I looked at the pictures by myself, I usually skipped the whole section about the crucifixion of Christ. I knew what was on those pages—the thief twisted in pain, the sad women kneeling at the foot of the cross where Jesus hung, his crown of thorns puncturing his brow, blood and water spurting from his side. That death didn't make sense.

Because Easter usually came before the roads to our own German church across the river opened up in spring, we often attended Easter services at the country Russian church. The Russians were friendly, generous people. On this special day, they brought the symbols of the risen Christ with them to the service—big mushroom-shaped loaves of decorated *paska* resting in baskets lined with colorfully embroidered napkins. When the people met on Easter Sunday, they greeted each other with special words—not "How are you?" or "Good morning" but with *"Christoss Voskress!"* (Christ is risen) to which the one being greeted responded, *"Voistinno Voskress"* (He has risen indeed). Occasionally the women would exchange *pysanky*, eggs painted in batik fashion with multi-colored design, as a symbol of the new life.

I couldn't say the Russian words, but the happy chorus of deep and high voices in the small, crowded entry, intermingled with human and sometimes barn smells, lifted the gloom of the previous days. I wished I could speak Russian so I could say the greeting to someone also. But always I was glad we could forget the terrible stories of Jesus on the cross for another year.

If my parents at times clung to Old Country customs, or at least enjoyed the *paska* and colored eggs, they found some of the new Canadian customs hard to accept. They had grown up in a country where the poor had actually begged door-to-door for food or starved. Therefore, they had no understanding of the custom of trick or treating at Halloween.

The first years we children asked to go out with our friends, Mother's answer was a firm "no" and Dad's even firmer. Go out begging? Unthinkable! No child of Dad's would beg for candy from his customers and friends. He would bring us candy from the store. We accepted the unpleasant ultimatum for several years, though we were bug-eyed with jealousy when our school friends came to the classroom the next morning burdened with candy kisses, gum, and apples, while we each cradled a little handful of suckers in one palm.

Every Halloween I went to Mother and Dad with the same request. I wanted to dress up like a ghost and go trick or treating. It wasn't begging, not the Russian kind where a boy or girl in tatters walked from door-to-door with soulful eyes, pleading for *Khleb* to keep from starving. We were in Canada, not Russia. It was fun, a kind of game. No one minded us children coming to their door for treats. Didn't Mother give cookies to the children who came to our door? Didn't Dad give gum and suckers to the children who came to the store? Couldn't I go, just once?

One year, after first talking it over with Dad in the little upstairs bedroom, Mother agreed to let me go with my friend Mona for "a little while." I found an old sheet, cut holes in it for eyes, and joined Mona and the other girls under the corner lightpost, a paper shopping bag under my arm. At last. I had made the break. I was one of the gang hollering "Trick or treat!" at door after door. Up one street and down another we went. We each collected a weighty bag of candy, gum, apples, and cookies. The butcher gave us each a wiener. The druggist handed out samples of toothpaste.

My "little while" was nearly used up when we knocked at a small white house, dimly lit, on a side street. I was shivering from the cold already and knew it was time to quit, but we wanted to finish off the last few houses before we went home to show off our loot to younger brothers and sisters.

I banged on the door of the small house with new-found bravado. I was doing it like the others, a real Canadian, no longer an immigrant, shouting "Trick or treat!" We never soaped anyone's windows if the people didn't give us treats, but that was what the other children always said, so we said it too. "Trick or treat!" we shrieked as we waited for someone to answer our knock.

A graying, thinnish woman with deep lines in her forehead, dressed in a limp, gingham housedress, opened the door. Brusquely she said, "There are no treats here tonight. A man is dying in here." She swung the door shut in my face.

My feet refused to move. Dying? How often had she said those words that evening? A man was dying behind the wooden door of the house with the low porch and the broken step. Was it her husband? Was he lying on the bed or sitting? What did people do when they knew they were dying? Did they talk about milking stools and ropes or about Halloween treats? Mona and I turned and went home, never saying a word. I never went trick or treating again.

Then one spring death moved close in another way. Next door to us lived an elderly couple named Zbitnoffs. I never figured out what Mr. Zbitnoff did for a living. I never figured out what many people in our small community did for a living if they didn't go to work on Main Street in one of the businesses there, like the grocery store, hardware, shoemaker shop, law office, drugstore, bank, cafe, or poolroom. I think Mr. Zbitnoff might have been a retired farmer. The congenial couple spoke too little English for me to understand their conversation with Mother, who spoke Russian well.

Mrs. Zbitnoff had a flourishing vegetable garden with lots more cabbage, dill, and cucumbers than we grew. We children ate the raspberries from the canes that grew over our side of the wooden fence. Our houses, built close together, looked almost like twins. If we had had windows on their side, I could have touched their wall with a long reach through a window—at least by using a short stick.

The long run alongside the house on our side of the

fence, closed off at one end by a rain barrel and a pile of wood, made a wonderful place to hide in the early evening when we children played Run, My Good Sheep, Run. Mrs. Zbitnoff often knew we were hiding there when we crouched next the galvanized iron rain barrel as she worked in her garden, but she never told on us. She only smiled her quiet, gentle smile while her eyes got lost in the crinkles of her skin.

One day Mrs. Zbitnoff told Mother that her daughter Glycera was coming home from her missionary work in North Africa. She was sick with that terrible disease tuberculosis. Tuberculosis (TB) meant first isolation, then surgery, then a slow death. The doctors in the East (meaning Toronto, always Toronto) had done the surgery, removing a lung and some ribs. She was coming home to die. Mrs. Zbitnoff's eyes glistened unusually brightly as she talked to Mother, who later relayed the story to us children.

Death was coming closer to me and our family. Next door. So close I could touch the trees, the rain barrel, and the house that would shelter it. My skin prickled at the thought.

We met Miss Z. several days later resting on her bed in the small front bedroom off the living room. She didn't mind us children staring at her and at the dozens of bottles and containers lined up on the small table—or even at her clothes lying on the patchwork quilt on her narrow bed.

I examined everything carefully, especially trying to get a good look at Miss Z. This dark-haired, dark-eyed woman with the thinned-out face and caved-in back and shoulders looked sick in her body, I decided, but her eyes looked alive and like a person who liked living. That seemed strange.

She joked and laughed and then spat into her paper sputum cups, which her mother burned almost immediately in the crackling flame of the kitchen stove. Sputum. I always liked the sound of the word. In Blaine Lake, lots of men spat, and the little globs, sometimes stained a deep tobacco brown, looked disgusting as they withered on the sidewalk on Main Street beside the dog turds. I watched carefully where I put my feet when I walked in front of the poolroom. But Miss Z.'s wasn't spit. It was sputum, and her mother burned it in the stove.

Signs of dying were all over her body, I thought to myself, if you looked hard enough. Paper-thin skin stretched over her high cheekbones. Her legs and arms were really skinny—like chopsticks. She had a strange, slow way of moving her body when she wanted to get up. Her clothes hung loosely, like a hundred-pound flour sack trying to cover only fifty pounds of the stuff.

The signs of death were there, but they had missed her eyes. Her eyes sparkled, as if daring death to overtake her. But then, maybe eyes were the last to die. Maybe someday I would walk over to her house, and her eyes would look like the rest of her or like the eyes of the minister in the coffin several years ago. I decided to watch her eyes; then I'd find out about death.

We girls visited her often in that small front bedroom of the next-door house. Miss Z. assured us there was no danger of catching TB. We should come as often as we liked. The sputum cup was an extra precaution because she had been a nurse.

As she lay in bed, she told us stories, always with a chuckle or the desire to amuse, about working in a hospital for natives in Africa. Another day she showed us how deeply corroded the underside of her wristwatch had become because of perspiring heavily in the tropics. We stood and marveled at the power of human sweat. In cold Saskatchewan we hardly knew what sweat was, even in summer.

She told us about the last trip home on the ship and how the ship's officers had wanted to carry her off the ship and to shore on a stretcher. She had refused. "As long as I can walk, I will." Sometimes we heard stories about growing up on a farm near Blaine Lake in the early pioneer days and of nurse's training in the city at a time when duty hours were long and strenuous. She brought a new dimension into our lives. She showed us a life of possibility beyond the borders of our small town even though her life was ending with TB. The previous years were worthwhile.

Then one day the sparkling eyes looked sad. We were paging through Eaton's mail-order catalog together, ooh-ing and ah-ing over the gorgeous lace-trimmed wedding dresses with long trains and beaded veils cascading down the brides' backs in billows of white airy foam. "I shouldn't be looking at wedding dresses," she commented to no one in particular. "I should be looking at funeral clothes." She spat out the remark like the men downtown spat out their chewing tobacco.

So death was coming after all. For a long time I didn't want to go next door anymore.

Shortly after Miss Z. returned to Blaine Lake, her father built a screened-in porch on the upstairs veranda. She wanted to sleep there in the open air, he told my mother. The doctors said it might help. He would humor her.

Each evening through the short summer and late into fall, when the snow was already falling gently in big feathery flakes on the dried grass and the air was getting crisp so that my nose tingled when I walked to school, Miss Z.'s mother wrapped her snugly in wool comforters with hot water bottles and heated bedstones. Then her mother rolled her cot onto the porch for the night.

Early, very early in spring, she started sleeping out there again. As I lay in my bed with Annie just a few feet from Miss Zbitnoff on the open porch, but separated now by only one wall and one screen, I thought about her. Glycera. A different name. Not like my plain one. A romantic name. I let it roll off my tongue.

There she lay alone on that veranda—always the last to

see the fireflies flitting in the night air, the first to check out the Big Dipper and to see the brilliant northern lights scramble through the heavens to find the best place to glimmer. In spring, she was the first to hear the rain dripping from the eaves, the first to smell the fresh breezes, the first to see the sun rising in the east, the first to hear the meadowlark greet the day. She was dying close to life, I decided. A rather nice way to go.

Glycera wore mules. I had seen the word in a storybook, so I knew what they were. Black satin ones, and a cotton dress that buttoned down the front to accommodate her weakened shoulder and arm muscles where the lung and bones had been cut out. As the months wore on, occasionally she walked to our house in her mules and cotton dress. She would enter through the kitchen door, sometimes going as far as the dining room to visit with Mother and drink a cup of tea. I decided she always carried her sputum cup with her so if death overtook her at an unguarded moment, she could cough its essence into the paper container and give it to someone to burn. I watched carefully for the day to come. Yet once again her eyes sparkled.

One Saturday Mother sent me to Zbitnoffs with some freshly baked crumbcake. I carried the plate carefully so as not to lose any of the buttery-crisp crumbs. Glycera was lying on her bed, dressed in a flowered navy silk dress—one without buttons marching down the front. The mules had been exchanged for solid black oxfords—low and comfortable. A new brown coat with a wolf-fur collar lay on her suitcases beside her. I looked so hard that I stumbled into the doorway and almost lost the cake.

She took the plate from me with a wide grin. Her mother smiled her usual crinkly smile, her dark eyes happy. Then Glycera reached down. Her eyes hugged me first. She stretched her arms out and drew me close. My hands felt the bones stick out and the hollow places gape as my arms closed around her cut-up body.

"I'm going to Toronto to visit some friends. Say thanks to your mother for the cake," she whispered. "I'll see you in fall. You helped me get well by visiting me."

I ran out the door and back home, not stopping to miss the cracks in the sidewalk as I usually did. My heart was singing. Glycera wasn't dying. She was going to live. I had looked into the darkness of the hole at the church graveyard that day when the woman was buried. I had seen death and been afraid. Glycera had stared into the darkness each night with those dark brown eyes and refused to let the darkness fill them. She had looked out, beyond the veranda screens, and had seen life.

Life was a gift, not a hostile force that tried to kill us off one by one. Grandmother Janzen in Russia had died lying on her thin mattress. She had struggled for life and to stay with those who had to milk the cows, but death had come. Yet there was a rhythm to life that included the limits of human strength to suffer and the potential of the human spirit to strike back. Glycera had looked up, night after night. She had found strength to die, and now she was going to live.

"*Christoss voskress,*" I shouted as I ran to tell Mother the good news. My plate was empty, yet Glycera had just given me a whole mountain of colored Easter eggs. And Easter was still two weeks away. I would listen to the Easter story this year. I understood.

"*Voistinno voskress! Voistinno voskress!*" shrilled a meadow lark on a fencepost.

17

Going Down Main Street

HOW MANY miles to Babylon?
Threescore miles and ten.
Can I get there by candlelight?
Yes, and back again.

I NEVER LIKED MY NAME when I was growing up. *Katie* began with a hard *K* and ended with a vowel that lent itself to being shrieked loudly and at great length when someone wanted me. It was an immigrant name—something brought along from South Russia. I was the first child born to my parents in the new land, but still I was handed an immigrant name. I was doomed to remain forever a Russian Mennonite peasant girl.

I agonized. Why hadn't my parents named me after a great writer or a prominent historical figure? I wanted something more glamorous than the simple Katie, which harkened back to a lowly beginning and to stories of unpleasant relatives nicknamed *Trien* and *Tienchen*, names used to tease me when I was grumpy. I wanted something classy—or at least a whole name like Katharina.

Instead, at my birth, my parents had fallen in step with the custom of their ethnic community, which picked only from a small list of traditional names like Henry, Peter, Jacob, John, Susie, Helen, and Annie. I don't think the Mennonites in South Russia had more than one or two dozen names in circulation. A child was frequently given the same name as a sibling who had died—and many children died in infancy. I considered my Russian-born forebears an uncreative lot. I wanted a name with flair.

"We were naming you Katharina," Mother told me. I checked my grandmother's handwritten family genealogy. Between 1865 and 1920, there were nine Katharina Funks, three by marriage, but no Katie. Katie was not Katharina.

"But you were named after them," Mother insisted.

"But I wasn't," I also insisted. There was no Katie among them. I wasn't a Katharina. My birth certificate name was Katie, plain as could be, which brought to mind images of black *Haube* (women's head coverings), *Schlorre*, and long, dark skirts. I must have had a birth defect to be forever saddled with Katie. It had no magic, no mystery to it, no association with greats of the past. I wanted to have a name like that of my school friends, whose names exuded romance and beauty. I wanted to be a June, Blanche, Fern, Kathleen, or Evelyn. I was oblivious to the fact that to cut myself off from the past was to risk hurting myself and my parents, for the past lives on in minds and bodies. But I was intent on doing so.

In late high school, I exchanged Katie for Kay, a name that seemed chic, modern, and more euphonious. For Christmas my sisters gave me a gold bracelet with Kay inscribed on it. It matched the sleek image I was developing for myself—long blonde pageboy, high heels, gloves that matched my scarf, lipstick when Dad wasn't watching, and boyfriends on the sly. I felt I could safely shed the past.

Mother had pushed the idea of us girls going on to high school. Fees were high—$15 for grades nine and ten, $20 for grade eleven, and $25 for grade twelve. Dad was not quite convinced when Frieda started high school that the future was brightest for his daughters if they got an education. Girls didn't need trigonometry and Latin when he had grown up.

But Mother won. I think he wanted it that way, for he admired the efficiency of the village clerk, a woman, and would have been pleased to have a daughter in that position. For such work, a person needed stenographic training.

Frieda had already left home for a nurse's training program. My sister Annie, now Anne with an "e," had gone to the city to normal school to become a teacher. Vocational opportunities for women at the time included nursing, teaching, and stenography. Our family had used up two options.

Nursing had never appealed to me like it did to Frieda, who had sometimes gone with our local doctor on his rounds. Teaching meant a country school with possibly thirty to forty children enrolled in all eight grades. When Anne the teacher came home for weekends, it seemed to me that teaching entailed mostly collecting pictures and making stacks of posters. It was too much like taking grade three all over again. In grade three my main aim in life was to find pictures of fruits and vegetables without words written over them. As a third grader, I scrounged through Dad's advertising posters which gave me the edge on my schoolmates who were limited to magazines. For years after I couldn't page through a magazine without commenting to myself how that complete picture of an apple would have looked on my grade three poster. Teaching seemed to be mostly collecting pictures. I said "no thanks" to that.

The third option of stenography seemed dull, forever limiting me to transcribing someone else's sentences, not creating my own. A fourth option—going to the university—was out of the question. No one in our family had done such a risky thing. Furthermore, a university degree didn't lead to an income. Money was scarce in our home. I peered ahead to life after high school and could see nothing.

Yet I prepared for my grade twelve final provincial examinations on which the entire year's grade depended because I enjoyed mastering academic material. Canada had been at war for three years. Teachers and students came and then went, particularly if male, to enlist in the army. For six weeks we had a teacher; the next day a new one. One day a classmate was not in his regular seat. But he reappeared in the middle of a literature class a few days later, in khaki uniform, grinning broadly, eager to exchange classroom boredom for the excitement of the war arena. Some never came back.

That final year in high school, I had four English literature teachers. The last one, Miss Drimmie, just fresh out of university, came for the concluding six weeks determined to redeem the lost year. She helped us grade twelve students study by going over old examinations. If there was solidarity in our agony, there was also unity in our attempts to ease the pain. Each evening we (eight students) got together to organize our material. We reviewed each course from beginning to end. I memorized nearly every poem in the English literature course from Shelley's "Ode to the West Wind" to Wordsworth's sonnets and the main speeches in Shakespeare's plays. I was ready for the provincial examiner. Often our study group ended up at the fairgrounds to sit on the bleachers, facing the empty ball field, wondering if any of us could hit a home run.

I earned one hundred points on the literature test and high grades in the other subjects. "Unbelievable," said my teacher, but the test graders were in Regina and not Blaine Lake, so she had to accept the grade as honestly earned.

Mother and Dad beamed when I won the Governor General's medal for our area. Dad was less pleased when I was notified that I would receive a small physics scholarship to the university. Because it was wartime, the university was not handing out any humanities scholarships. Dad had no resources to put up the rest of the money for university. The offer made him uncomfortable.

Somehow the decision was made that I would attend a

technical institute to learn to type and write shorthand, despite my teacher's advice that I was intended for bigger things. I would become a stenographer. Coming out of the Russian experience followed by the Depression, my parents convinced me it was more important to find a way to earn a living than to make a life. I denied my potential because I didn't know how to acknowledge it without money. I fell in step with their expectations. As I see it now, my parents and I had limited choices at the time because there were no women role models in the field of writing.

The day I left Blaine Lake for the technical institute to learn to become a stenographer, the car stood outside the door packed with my few belongings and the various items I needed for light housekeeping—eggs, pancake flour, and cans of beans and spaghetti. The omnipresent store followed me to the city. An ungainly Toronto couch was tied to the roof of the car. Dad had made arrangements for me to live with a Russian family in their spare bedroom. I used the window ledge as a refrigerator, a two-burner kerosene stove for cooking, and an orange crate cupboard for storing dishes. I was nearly eighteen.

The packed car was too small for the family to come along. Mother, Jack, and Susie stayed home. Jakie was now Jack and Susie was on the way to becoming Susan. After a quick breakfast, Dad and I were ready to leave. I walked out the door, confident, ready for the new adventure, armed with a fierce independence. I had always been independent, refusing to ask for help if I struggled with a knitting pattern or a trigonometry assignment. In that I was like Dad, who could never lower himself to ask for directions when traveling. You never admitted defeat. Stenography wouldn't faze me.

As I walked out the door, the radio played, "Be not dismayed, whate'er betide; God will take care of you." I cried. Mother wiped her hands on her apron, then she cried. I didn't want to go down Main Street to the city.

Would I ever again hear the clock insistently chiming the quarter hours? The familiar sounds of the family breathing and coughing at night? Nails popping from the frost? Wind howling around the corner? The fire crackling gently in the stove and a log falling? A piece of ice letting go of the edge and slipping into the tank?

Would I ever hear again horses' hooves clip-clopping down the hard-packed snow, sleigh bells ringing merrily, and little boys, bundled to their nose tips, shouting loudly while playing hockey with frozen horse turds on slick streets? I was saying good-bye to the familiar sounds of the blacksmith neighbor getting ready to put a rim on a wagon wheel, people walking downtown on wooden sidewalks and stopping to greet one another below my window.

Would I ever again wake-up hearing the early crow of the rooster welcoming the day? Or walk briskly for an early morning piano lesson with Mrs. Davidson, who lived next door, stopping to greet a newly arrived robin?

Gone forever were the high school socials, with a committee who made lists of who would bring what and who once again would cajole some innocent fellow student into letting the class use his mother's copper washboiler. For each party the student had to be someone who didn't know that the valuable boiler would be placed over an open fire to heat water for coffee and would come back sooty and banged up.

Being a princess at the winter carnival now seemed something out of the distant past, not just last winter. The girl with the most votes had been crowned queen and the other two named princesses. I had had no courage to go door-to-door to sell votes for myself. Selling yourself was not a Mennonite thing. So I had to be satisfied with a princess role, a blue crepe-paper tiered gown, and a flat, frilly headpiece tied with a huge bow under my chin—all worn over a heavy snowsuit, resulting in chunky royal attendants. The queen wore a crepe-paper ermine cape.

Never again would I "walk the tracks." In spring, every teenager with red blood flowing in his or her veins took to the tracks, for they were the only area clear of snow. You went walking with whoever might be interested in you, if only with your girlfriend. Mona Stuart was my girlfriend and Sam, her brother, wanted to be my boyfriend.

The Stuarts lived across the alley from us in a large, dark gray, weathered two-story house, which housed the local weekly newspaper on the lower floor. The Stuarts were a family I never understood, only enjoyed. The family was never fully accepted in Blaine Lake, probably because of Mr. Stuart's open socialist views. The Stuarts were British and had moved much in comparison to our settled life in Blaine Lake. Mr. Stuart, editor of *The Blaine Lake Echo*, was educated. My father had little or no formal schooling. We never knew much about the Stuarts' past but sensed they derived from a wealthy family in England from which they had possibly been ousted.

The Stuarts' food was as different from ours as chitlins and collards are from roast beef and mashed potatoes. They ate such strange things as jam pie and Yorkshire pudding. We relished big pots of borscht, plates of *Vereniki* and *Portzelchi*. Their home was papered with yellowing, water-stained newsprint; every wall, nook and cupboard in our home was painted with several coats of high-gloss enamel.

But their large family of girls and boys our age brought together two uninhibited strains of creativity, love of beauty, and openness of spirit. They enjoyed a strange mixture of inner wealth and outer poverty. On Saturdays, Sam pulled handset type apart while listening to the Metropolitan Opera. Sometimes we joined him. That became our practice for years thereafter.

On summer afternoons, if we wanted the Stuart children to come out to play, we spread all the proofsheets of *The Echo* on the office counter. Everyone picked a page to proofread. With the Stuarts we sang around their tiny heater in their skimpily furnished upstairs living quarters or went on a nature jaunt. They showed me that poverty doesn't need to rob you of dignity or imagination. Would those carefree Saturday afternoons ever return?

Or that wonderful summer when we invented our own language? Frieda's Russian orchestra leader had been teaching the players Esperanto, the international artificial language. Who could forbid us from also inventing our own language, which only we children could understand? For several days Frieda and Annie had made booklets with glossaries of nouns, verbs, adjectives, and adverbs. They called the new language Esperene. I remember only one word—*alba*, for *ass*. We used it to excess, for it allowed us to use a vulgarism without Mother knowing what we were giggling about. We were limited to expletives like "swell," "lousy," and "gee." No "heck," or "darn," and certainly no "ass" in ordinary discourse to refer to a body part. All that would be left behind when we drove down Main Street.

Where was that other world, my secret world, the world no one knew about? Twilight had become for me that precious time to spend alone outside, sitting on the woodpile or the backstep, for a few last moments. If I was inside, I relaxed in the high-back rocker with a patchwork cushion, wondering and dreaming. Twilight was the time for finding and listening to the silence within. Where would I fit in? What would I be doing? Would I be a writer like Jo (what a dashing name!) in *Little Women*?

My childhood memories came stumbling toward me to say good-bye. Before I stepped into the car, Dad silently sneaked me a wristwatch. We left. Down Main Street. For the city. For the new life.

Years later I made a pilgrimage back to Blaine Lake, to the house with the fence and gate, to the store with the same wrinkled, green shade. Mother and Dad had long ago moved to a warmer climate. My own life had changed.

The west wind had blown across my spirit and, like my father, I had heard the Spirit speaking. That question had been settled. I knew whom I belonged to. I had begun to see that stenography was not a dead end. But sometimes that other business, that immigrant business, still bothered me. It crouched at my feet, wrapping its tentacles around my ankles, preventing me from moving freely. I wanted to be able to write about all kinds of ideas, but always I found my father's stories interrupting me.

That day on that return pilgrimage to Blaine Lake, you were not in the store, Dad, but I saw your image behind the counter, standing there in your sand-colored smock, adding up the day's receipts. I wanted to blurt out, "Dad, you made me a Mennonite when you gave me the name of one. You had the chance here in Blaine Lake to pass us off as Russians or Germans, but you didn't take it. You loaded Mennonitism on us. You seduced me with your stories of a people enduring hardship.

"I want to believe all of it. I want that kind of faith that suffered courageously and endured to the end. But now I also find some of what you found in the church in Russia—loveless power and powerless love. Dad, you escaped the bonds of the past, and even the present, by living here in Blaine Lake all these years. You could observe the situation from afar. But I've married into it. How do I reconcile my confusion? I can't get out.

"Dad, what do I do with this craving inside me to write—to wrap my experiences in words to let others see them? Didn't you ever feel anything like that? You told us never to forget we were Funks. What did you mean by that?"

Then came the real issue. The words were pouring out. "Why didn't you and Mother ever give me a real name? You called me Katie—a peasant name, not a writer's name, not a name for this land. And I have to use it all the time, exposing my past. You offered me the freedom of living in Blaine Lake, but at the same time you wrapped around me a heavy chain forged by your own experiences.

Dad wasn't there in the store or in the warehouse or even in your tiny office at the back or in the basement with its stacks of canned goods and piles of empty cartons. How many hours had we spent together in the store? Why did I resist his legacy?

I left the store and walked down Main Street, past the dry-goods store owned by the village's only Jew, past the drugstore where we bought our medicine, past the cafe once owned by a Chinese proprietor, around the train station where we departed and returned so often during the war years. Then I walked slowly down the other side, past the hotel, the pool hall, the hairdresser, the butcher shop, the other pool hall where we always slowed down to catch a glimpse of the sin that was supposed to be lurking in its dark corners. I walked past the bank with the benches in front where the local unemployed and retired men rested. Everything was nearly as it had been.

Then I heard a voice whispering above the rattle and roar of cars and trucks looking for parking spots. "I did give you a name, Katie, child of the prairies, child of the Russian steppes, child of many sojournings. But your name, being the gift of others, must be made your own. You didn't select your parents, your race, or your name, but you have to choose what you make of your Blaine Lake experiences and those of your parents and of their parents and of all those who wandered, sometimes fruitlessly, in search of freedom. Sometimes that search ended in failure. Sometimes it succeeded.

"It was a triumph of the spirit when those individuals accepted the gift of their heritage—the weaknesses, faults, mistakes, as well as the conquests, strengths, and joys—and gleaned from all what they needed to move ahead with courage."

Then I remembered one of your last letters, Dad. You wrote, "Yes, Katie, I made many mistakes in life. You only get experience after you have lived, but you need it before you live. And that is why a person makes mistakes. When I look back, I ask myself, why didn't I do it differently? Why didn't I? That is a question I can't answer. All I know is that I didn't have the experience to do it differently with the little education I had. Life isn't fair. Life is a struggle."

So you too sometimes wondered about your past.

As I walked down the last block, past the service station to turn toward the school, the dinginess of the community lifted. I could see it in a new way. *Life is a struggle, not a slippery slide.* The dirt road on which Dad and I drove away on that September morning was now graveled. *Why didn't I do it differently?* The sign at the end of the street pointed to the highway. *You only get experience after you have lived.* Dad, you gave me the privilege of reliving your life with you when you shared your memories with me.

I embraced my roots—the Russian-German ones and those grafted in by this variegated community in which I had lived almost eighteen years. My chains fell loose at my feet. My ancestors had not been complacent, accepting blindly what others told them to believe about God, life, and themselves. They had chosen. They had made mistakes. Mother and Dad had chosen a new way of living in a new country. That was their gift to me. I too could choose.

Other girls could be Kay, Kae, Katherine, Kathryn, Kathleen, Kaylene, and Kathy. I left town bearing the name Katie proudly. It may have been the name of a peasant. But now it was my name. I had chosen it. And my past.

Author

Katie Funk Wiebe, professor emeritus at Tabor College, retired in 1990 after teaching English for twenty-four years. She attended the Mennonite Brethren Bible College in Winnipeg for two years and is a graduate of Tabor College (B.A.) and Wichita State University (M.A.). She is now working as a freelance writer and editor.

In addition to hundreds of articles, Wiebe has written and/or edited fourteen books, focused recently on aging. Her most recent book is *Border Crossing: A Spiritual Journey* (Herald Press, 1995). Other books with an aging theme include *Prayers of an Omega: Facing the Transitions of Aging* (Herald Press, 1994); *Life after Fifty: A Positive Look at Aging in the Faith Community* (Faith & Life, 1993); *Bless Me Too, My Father* (Herald Press, 1988); *Good Times with Old Times: How to Write Your Memoirs* (Herald Press, 1979); and *Older Adults and Faith: Making New Maps* (Faith & Life, 1995).

Among earlier books are *Alone: A Search for Joy* (Tyndale, 1976, Kindred Press, 1987) *Who Are the Mennonite Brethren?* (Kindred Press, 1984) and *Women Among the*

Brethren (General Conference of Mennonite Brethen Churches, 1979). She was a columnist for the *Christian Leader* for thirty years. She has also written four adult Bible study guides. She was editor of *Rejoice!*, the inter-Mennonite devotional guide, for nearly five years and continues as a workshop and retreat leader.

Wiebe grew up in northern Saskatchewan, the daughter of Russian-German immigrants. In the Funk home, storytelling was part of the family tradition. She moved to Kansas in 1962. She attends the First Mennonite Brethren Church in Wichita.

She has traveled to India, Bangladesh and Nepal, the former Soviet Union, Europe, and Central America.

She is a member of the Peace Education Commission of the United States Mennonite Brethren Conference and of the board of the Center for Mennonite Brethren Studies in Hillsboro, Kansas. She has four children and five grandchildren.